THE 'SPECIAL' T

MW00877330

ALAN CUMBERLAND was principal timpanist of the London Philharmonic Orchestra from 1968 to 1987. In 1987 he was appointed as Senior Lecturer in Percussion/Timpani at the Queensland Conservatorium and Principal of the Young Conservatorium, a position he held for eleven years before relocating to Hong Kong where from 1998 to 2015 he was Head of Woodwind, Brass and Percussion and Resident Conductor of the Symphony Orchestra at the Hong Kong Academy for Performing Arts. In 2004 he published the trilogy of books *20 Graduated Studies for Timpani*, *Two Challenges for Timpani* and *11 Graduated Studies for Snare Drum*.

THE 'SPECIAL' TIMPANIST

ALAN CUMBERLAND

Edited by
BRETT CARVOLTH

Foreword by
SIMON CARRINGTON

THE SPECIAL TIMPANIST
Copyright © 2014 by ALAN CUMBERLAND
Edited by BRETT CARVOLTH 2017

All Rights reserved. No Part of this publication may be reproduced, stored in a retrieval system, or transmitted in any form or by any means, electronic, mechanical, photocopying, recording, or otherwise, without the prior permission of both the copyright owner and publisher of this book.

Book and Cover design by BRETT CARVOLTH

ISBN-13: 978-1541383500
ISBN-10: 1541383508

First Edition: May 2017

Edited by
BRETT CARVOLTH

Brett Carvolth was born in Brisbane in 1969. He studied with Alan
Cumberland at the Queensland Conservatorium graduating with a
Bachelor of Music in 1990. Brett has performed and toured with many
ensembles and artists throughout Australia, New Zealand and Asia. A
composer and arranger of works for percussion he has more than thirty
years' experience in music education and has a keen interest in percussion
instrument manufacture and design.

ACKNOWLEDGEMENTS

This book was written by Alan Cumberland in September 2014. All opinions expressed are those of the author. Comments made within are not intended to offend, with the exception of those relating to a well-known bald Hungarian man. Most are mere observations of the respective individuals' talent or in some cases, a distinct lack thereof.

Inspiration for this book was drawn from Alan's illustrious career working with some of the world's finest soloists and conductors. A collection of charismatic, interesting and gifted musicians, many of which he regarded as close friends.

Alan's unique sense of humour provided numerous occasions where colleagues found themselves entangled in circumstances often described as, somewhat *"unfortunate"*. There are too many to list here, however, brief mention should be made of the following for their participation (*sometimes unwillingly*):

Keith Millar, Peter Chrippes, John Cobb, Nigel Thomas,
E Gerald Kirby, Jeremy Cornes and Geoff Prentice.

Special thanks to Sandy Leung, Jan Judson, Helen Cumberland, Annette and Lisa for their endless love and support.

Thanks also to Brett Carvolth *(Editor)*, Simon Carrington *(Foreword)*, Craig Dabelstein for proof reading and Raymond Vong for his assistance in the preparation of musical examples and photos.

Sincere thanks to Gus Christie and family, Glyndebourne, East Sussex.

To the hundreds of former students from the Royal College of Music, Queensland Conservatorium and Hong Kong Academy for Performing Arts, Alan's legacy continues through you.

"LIFE IS FOR LIVING"

For

Chloe
&
Ella

This book is dedicated to my many students who are now in prominent positions in major symphony orchestras around the world with whom it has been such a pleasure to work and who continue to 'spread the word'.

Just a few of these special musicians are

David Arnold

Andy Barclay

Tony Bedewi

Simon Carrington

Brett Carvolth

John Chimes

Polly Chimes

Tim Corkeron

Jeremy Cornes

Elizabeth Davis

Kate Eyre

Peter Fry

Martin Gibson

Lucas Gordon

Steve Webberley

Troy Greatz

Kevin Hathway

David Hext

Russell Jordan

Gerald Kirby

Andrew Knox

Rick Parmigiani

Neil Percy

Geoff Prentice

Larry Reese

David Stirling

Nigel Thomas

Alex Timcke

Raymond Vong

CONTENTS

LIST OF ILLUSTRATIONS
Pages 48 – 68

LIST OF MUSICAL EXAMPLES
Alphabetical by Composer

FOREWORD
by
SIMON CARRINGTON

Everyone who met Alan Cumberland recognised that he was a rare breed; as well as being a wonderful musician and hugely inspiring teacher he was a unique personality, throughout his years on this earth genuinely fascinated and amused by the world and its inhabitants. He made an impression everywhere he went, whether as timpanist for the London Philharmonic Orchestra from 1968 - 87 or in his capacity as teacher, conductor and administrator in Australia and Hong Kong after he left the orchestral profession.

I first became aware of Alan in 1982 when my Hampshire friend and mentor, the dearly departed percussionist Chris Guy suggested coming to hear "Alan Cumberland, the best timpanist in the world" play at the Royal Festival Hall with the London Philharmonic Orchestra. It was Mahler's 3rd Symphony, conducted by one of the eminent conductors of the day – I don't recall his name, or where he was from, only that he had a bald head, an extremely unfriendly demeanour and twitched and convulsed on the podium like some kind of demented ostrich. It matters not, for all that was important to me was the experience of listening to a great orchestra play some wonderful music. Alan was a complete inspiration to watch and to listen to, and even at my young age, knowing absolutely nothing about any of it I was struck by the mixture of power and subtlety with which he played, allied to his natural and so beautifully musical approach, always blending with the sound of the orchestra.

I was totally hooked from that moment on and in due course was lucky enough to have a consultation lesson with Alan at the Royal College of Music. I remember that first lesson well, anticipating it with some trepidation: what would he say about my technique and how I played – would he just dismiss everything and make me start again from scratch? I need not have worried; Alan placed a Delecluse study on the music stand and just said "How about playing this for me?". I gave it a go, he made a few suggestions about phrasing and emphasis and in so doing opened my eyes and ears to the possibilities of simply playing the timpani in a relaxed, musical and melodic manner – revolutionary!

Alan said that he was happy to teach me on an ongoing basis, thus I joined a long line of people that were privileged to study with him over many years. His primary attribute as a teacher was to lead by example; he never tried to impose his own way, rather he encouraged what was natural to each student and gave them confidence whilst conveying his own love of music and the timpani in his characteristically wonderful and enthusiastic manner. The list of people to whom this book is dedicated is a direct testament to Alan's inspiration as player and teacher and there are of course countless other people, from all walks of life the world over that were also lucky enough to benefit from his amazing wit, wisdom and warmth during his lifetime.

In the pages of this book is the story of a man who simply loved music, musicians and life and who maintained, throughout what can be an extremely arduous profession an unparalleled sense of humour as well as a supreme ability to inspire those around him. I feel sure that anyone reading this book will laugh out loud at the way Alan describes the various situations in which he found himself over the years. I am also sure that readers will be fascinated by his insight about all matters relating to music and the music profession, timpani and timpani playing, orchestras, and of course the conductors who influenced his life in all sorts of ways, sometimes for the better and sometimes for the much, much worse.

It is a great privilege for me to be invited to contribute to this book and Brett Carvolth and Alan's family are to be thanked and congratulated for collating Alan's writings, musings and photos, thus honouring his wish that for the benefit ,edification and amusement of everybody they are available to enjoy, in perpetuity.

Perhaps more than anything his words will be provide us with a glimpse of what lay at the centre of Alan Cumberland the musician and will help to crystallise some of the extraordinary qualities, musical and otherwise that made him such a unique and genuinely "special" timpanist.

Simon Carrington
May 2017

"The Special Timpanist"
(Photo by Peter Musson 1988)

Part One

THE 'SPECIAL' TIMPANIST

This book is not a manual on how to play the timpani or instructions about what you *must* do to become a successful timpanist (there are too many books like this). It is a combination of a short biography, some pointers in the basics and interpretation of timpani parts together with some true stories about the days in the life of just one professional timpanist. Please enjoy. Remember,

"LIFE IS FOR LIVING"

The Beginning

I was born in Luton, a rather insignificant town around thirty miles north of London, with an under-achieving football team. It still is. Dad used to take me every other Saturday to watch the home games. We stood behind the goal and always had plenty of space around us as when the cross came over from the wings, he would head or kick the imaginary ball into the net. Fellow supporters gave him a wide berth to avoid bruised shins or being head-butted. Mum was at home trying on a couple of dozen ridiculous hats that Dad, a milliner by trade, had brought from his work so she could wear a different one each Sunday in church. She was asked on one occasion by a member of the congregation sitting behind her, who was preaching, as they could not see the pulpit.

Dad dabbled on the piano and piano accordion (!!!) whilst Mum enjoyed singing pretending to be Kathleen Ferrier. It was obvious quite early on that I had some kind of "ear" for music as with the passing of the steam train some way off, I would go to the piano and play the same note as the whistle, just as I did when Dad blew his nose a couple of octaves lower.

Starting the piano between the ages of four and five was good for me as it kept me out of mischief. The challenge of playing everything given to me by my dear old lady teacher at breakneck speed was too great to ignore. Still unable to reach the pedals, music festivals and competitions began to feature in my life.

Such was the interest created by the piano, my parents were keen to add a second string to my bow, as it were, by introducing the violin. I hated it at first as the pitch of the notes had to be determined by me, but was encouraged by my elderly gentleman teacher. He wore carpet slippers, in and out. It wasn't uncommon for the alternative carpet slipper, a *ppp* one, to almost inaudibly ease its way out of his rear passage into the unventilated teaching room. As I progressed, I couldn't wait to play such masterpieces as Monti's *Czardas*, hoping desperately I wouldn't overshoot the first high A on the G string. Scales and arpeggios are as we all know, a complete waste of time, so to save it, I used to "practice" them at my weekly lessons. This didn't go down too well with my teachers. Later I realised that if I didn't work at them slowly, I could never guarantee that octave leap and other positional changes.

I suppose I was around ten years old when my parents decided I should move on, so I applied to the Guildhall School of Music & Drama and was awarded a place as a junior exhibitioner. Every Saturday morning, Dad took me on the 7.00am train up to London and left me there to study piano, violin and other boring things like history, harmony and musical appreciation. I loved aural, 'cos I could do it. I was also in the orchestra as a violinist. Later on, Dad decided I was old and responsible enough to make the journey on my own. I was at that age when exploring was the thing to do. Who wanted to play scales and run through the same monotonous pieces with the orchestra every week? I soon discovered that after leaving the train at St Pancras, instead of taking the bus, I could find my way to the underground and the circle line, get on and sit there going round and around, carefully timing my exit back at the main line station to coincide with the train back to Luton. Now this was far more interesting than ploughing through Mozart's *Ave Verum Corpus* and the first movement of Schubert's *Unfinished*. My parents were blissfully unaware of this until they saw one of my reports which read "too many missed lessons for progress". Somehow, I managed to wriggle out of that one.

To spice up my music a little more, the organ was introduced. The organ! This instrument was even worse, in that not only the pitch was fixed, but it was all but impossible, for me anyway, to incorporate any kind of dynamics or phrasing. To compound matters further, I was expected to simultaneously play a different line with my feet. But I persevered and "practiced", which meant opening up all the stops and the doors in the church just across from our house which had kindly been made available to me by the vicar. I soon lost interest.

Around the age of thirteen, my parents persuaded me to apply for the National Youth Orchestra (NYO) of Great Britain. This I did and was accepted on violin for the following 'course'. Having practised (for real this time) my parts, I was ready. Upon arrival at the school, I was told the founder, Dr Ruth Railton wanted to see me. What had I done wrong before the course had even begun? Apart from suggesting my hair could do with a spot of Brylcreem (I took her advice and plastered great dollops of the stuff on my hair for the next time she saw me) she advised me that the violin section had its full complement of players, but I was expected to step up in the case of an emergency. "Would you mind, therefore, if you sat at the back of the orchestra, as a "general musician" with our percussion players to make the most of your chance to learn and work with some of the world's finest instrumentalists and conductors?" "Oh, what a wonderful opportunity and privilege, Dr Railton. Thank you so much".

It was at this meeting I met a cellist, Nigel Pinkett. Nigel and I soon realised we had much in common and have enjoyed acting with diminished responsibility for countless years as well as being life-long friends.

Where it all started

During the course, the tutor of the percussion section asked if I would be interested in "having a go", so I did. I was also given the chance to play in some of the concerts (on the least damaging instruments such as triangle, bass drum and gong). All too easy, I thought. This is something different. I had my own instrument and did not have to share the same part with twenty-three other players. And so I was happy sitting at the back watching and listening as the violinists struggled with thousands of notes. It was compulsory for everyone to stay in the hall for the duration of the rehearsals and my only difficulty was to avoid nodding off, especially when the be-cloaked Dr Railton was lurking. As each and every course went by, I was "developing" into an orchestral percussionist rather than a violinist. I would have loved the opportunity to try the timpani, but that coveted position was already accounted for. Much fun was had with the NYO thrice annually, working with outstanding musicians, making new friends and travelling the world.

By this time, I had transferred to Dunstable Grammar School where my performance from an academic standpoint was unremarkable. On occasions, it slipped below what my teachers would call an acceptable and manageable level. My music on the other hand dominated on a limited scale with regular appearances at school and local concerts playing solos on violin and piano. There is not much more to be said about my contribution to DGS. It was the tradition for all graduating boys to meet with the headmaster before leaving the school. The dreaded L. P. Banfield signalled for me to enter his study where he said, "Cumberland, you seem to have achieved precious little at this school, save your music. Do you honestly expect to make any reasonable kind of living out of classical music? I think not. Whatever you choose, however, I wish you well. Goodbye". I shook his hand and said "thank you sir" and thought "miserable old bastard".

So having left school at the earliest opportunity, I was faced with a "gap" year before being eligible to start at the Royal College of Music (RCM), where I was fortunate enough to have been offered a double major scholarship on piano and violin. That year was spent as a junior clerk in the cost office of the Eastern Electricity Board (EEB). How anyone could possibly spend their whole working life in those surroundings is totally beyond me. I wanted fun, enjoyment and above all, my music. There wasn't a lot at the EEB. Every evening, I listened to classical music, mainly opera, on the transistor radio at my bedside.

Having survived that year of abject boredom, it was time to move to the big smoke. This meant leaving home and finding somewhere to live. This was new and exciting. Taking in as much as I could on orientation day at the college, I noticed that there were three orchestras: Sir Adrian Boult was the conductor of the first, then came the second, and the third was for first-years and "others". I was somewhat taken aback to see my name (well down the order of violins) in the first orchestra and then even more so when on the third orchestra list I saw "timpani: Alan Cumberland". I went straight to the office to let them know that I had never even sat behind a set of timpani before, let alone played them. The nice man there said he knew I had played some percussion, "so you must know something about timpani. There is nobody else—you are the timpanist".

So there it was, the first time to sit behind four large copper bowls. I suppose it was akin to driving a bus rather than a car. I didn't even have any sticks, so I borrowed them from the junior school. Reading the music was of course no problem and the pitching of different notes was of no real concern even though the tuning at that time was a manual rather than a bipedal operation. A large part of the repertoire for timpani requires the player to produce a roll, which normally means that one stick follows closely after the other. This was somewhat problematic as when my sticks tended to strike the drum simultaneously (which they frequently did) it was rather difficult to get them back to go left, right, left, right without stopping. I persevered though and began to enjoy the experience. At the same time I was on the fiddle in the main orchestra which on one occasion was in F minor, struggling through Tchaikovsky 4. This work contains a rather important timpani part which requires precise tuning. The person at the back was clearly aurally challenged on that day and I was desperate to "get up there".

The authorities at Prince Consort Road knew of my desire and suggested I have some lessons with Henry Taylor, the former timpanist of the London Symphony Orchestra (LSO). A few weeks later, after consulting with Mr Taylor, the same kind gentleman in the office informed me that they would like me to continue with timpani/percussion lessons, but as I was already on a "double major", something had to go. They strongly recommended that I retained the piano (a decision that turned out to be exactly right) leaving violin as the casualty. They gave me a few days to think about it before my parents were called up for a chat. My mind was clearly made up but it took a while to convince them that this was what I wanted, so they reluctantly agreed. This was the best decision I ever made. I can just imagine what it must be like to sit at the back of the violins in an orchestra day in, day out, assuming that is, if I made it into an orchestra in the first place. It was in my first term at the college, that the very same gentleman who had managed my "switch" from violin to percussion called me to ask if I was interested in performing at the National Theatre. I was to be one of Fortinbras' musicians in the inaugural production of *Hamlet* at the Old Vic. Naturally I jumped at it and found myself on the same stage as Sir Laurence Olivier, Max Adrian, Peter O'Toole, Sir Michael Redgrave, Joan Plowright, Derek Jacobi, Christopher Timothy, Maggie Smith, Michael Gambon, John Stride and a host of others. A little later on I was one of four personal musicians and choristers for Sir Laurence in Congreve's *Love for Love* where I played a variety of percussion instruments (especially adapted so I could carry them around on stage) and the solo pianist for Sir Laurence again as he danced Strindberg's famous *Dance of Death* with Geraldine McEwan miming it on stage. I loved the theatre. What an incredible experience. Needless to say, I did not appreciate it at the time and simply took it all for granted.

Idiot!

As well as the cellist in the National Theatre, Nigel was a student at RCM when we shared a flat in south London. The evening's orchestral concert on one day promised to be a rather dull affair, so we decided to brighten up the occasion by placing four or five small tablets (readily available from the joke shop in Soho) at regular intervals along the lower ground floor corridor towards the gent's toilet. Around fifteen minutes before the concert was due to begin, the pellets were ignited and magically transformed without flames or smoke into a shape that strikingly resembled something in which one would not choose to tread, or indeed have on one's shoes whilst listening to a Vaughan Williams' symphony. We heard one regular concert-goer say to the caretaker, "Mr. Brown, has your dog been downstairs?"

Jobs were coming in thick and fast. It was around this time that after two second-hand cars, I had taken delivery of my first brand new vehicle—a Volvo 144, yes, a Volvo, because my mother insisted *"that it is the safest vehicle on the road"*. When passing through Dunstable one day, I took the opportunity to drive this pitifully slow machine back to the school and popped in to let Mr Banfield know that I was just managing to make ends meet. So slow was this car that I was forced to learn the art of heel-to-toe braking to save vital seconds when shifting down, a technique that proved invaluable later when pedaling upon the timpani.

I left the RCM without qualifications after a year as I was far too busy playing in all manner of ensembles and had no time to further my studies. One such ensemble was when three colleagues and I were engaged to play military drums in elaborate costume and march in line with trumpets, accompanied by jugglers, dancers and others through the streets of London to celebrate the start of Italian week in Britain. The route was to take us across Westminster Bridge, around Parliament Square then directly to Buckingham Palace and back again. After a short briefing in one of Westminster City Councils' offices, we had ninety minutes or so to spare before the pageant began and so adjourned to the nearest hostelry for a pint or two. After assembling back at City Hall for the start, we donned our heavy costumes and instruments and waited in line in Belvedere Road for the cue to get going. This took some time and was uncomfortable as it was very warm. Then we were off. *Now you know what is coming, and you'd be right!* Many people were lining the route and all traffic had been stopped. As we approached the Houses of Parliament it became clear to us that a visit to the pub before such an event was not such a good idea after all. We shouted options to each other as we marched and decided upon the best plan of action. Well before reaching Westminster station, two of us peeled off to the right, significantly stepping up our tempo (but still playing and maintaining that of the band) to the nearby underground public conveniences, leaving the other two to hold the fort. At the stalls, the sticks were held fast under one armpit as both hands were required to locate and undo the large brass buttons positioned underneath the heavy drum. We needed one hand to keep the fly open and the other to hold our "parts". Elbows and wrists were used in conjunction to keep the instrument out of the line of fire. As luck would have it, as we were doing our business, the marchers were negotiating Parliament Square so we cancelled that part of the parade and stuck to the main road, rejoining them just a short distance ahead. We swapped positions in the line and our two remaining colleagues then sidled off following the same routine and with a quick march caught up with the body of the group somewhere down Birdcage Walk. Everybody was having such a great time, nobody noticing a thing.

I soon became timpanist of Harry Blech's London Mozart Players and for Yehudi Menuhin with his then Bath Festival Orchestra. It was with Yehudi that I recorded *The Soldier's Tale* for Thames TV. Offers of work with different orchestras followed, including the London Symphony, with whom I was the regular number 4 perc (this was thanks to the principal Jimmy Holland, who stood by me despite an embarrassing moment at the Royal Festival Hall (RFH) with Colin Davis. I was playing the castanets in Britten's *Young Person's Guide* when during the solo, the instruments somehow became detached from my fingers and the resulting clattering noise resembled the gnashers of Reginald Rashleigh, an elderly colleague with ill-fitting dentures). It was one of Reg's even more elderly friends who, when the conductor yelled "tambourine LATE", uttered the famous words, "well it left *here* on time".

On one occasion at RFH with the LSO waiting for the orchestral manager to call us back to the stage to resume the rehearsal for the symphony, I thought I would liven up the atmosphere. I reached into my pocket to find a soft plastic puffer of sneezing powder. I casually walked by the bench where the conductor was sitting and squeezed more than once. I retreated to a safe distance before hearing a few spluttering noises coming from his direction. The typical pre-sneezing gasps quickly turned into snorts and then into the reaching, convulsing sounds that only Japanese people can make. It was poor Seiji Ozawa streaming from the nose and eyes, with similarly affected members of the orchestra armed with tissues to help him along. It did have the desired effect in that the rehearsal resumed some ten minutes late. A similar incident occurred as Sir Laurence Olivier was preparing to make a speech to thank the sponsors and patrons of the Shakespeare Trust for inviting the National Theatre to perform at Shakespeare's birthplace in Stratford-upon-Avon. After the actions of Nigel and myself, he too struggled for breath as he suffered with incessant nasal explosions for some minutes before he was able to form a word. We were of course at the back of the reception room sympathizing with him and the accompanying dignitaries wondering what on earth could have caused this unpleasant experience.

The Royal Philharmonic subsequently invited me to become sub-principal percussionist, which I enjoyed immensely with Keith Millar as the principal. I occasionally played timpani, which despite the Premier drums, I loved. Nigel was also in the Royal Philharmonic Orchestra (RPO) at this time where orchestral breaks and meals were again disrupted, this time with tear gas from a small glass phial. The tip of the glass was broken off and the clear liquid deposited at various points along the bar. We used a similar ploy in an Italian restaurant in Earl's Court where, after returning from the gents, left a trail at the far end near the kitchen and returned to our seats by the window. We could soon see handkerchiefs and serviettes being put to good use as patrons were systematically forced out of their seats in their search for fresh air as the invisible toxic fumes spread throughout the restaurant. Mario the waiter was dancing about frantically waving a menu in a desperate attempt to increase the circulation. To prevent any more foul air getting in, the diners insisted he should not attempt to open the windows, which was futile as they were in fact stuck fast with grease. The noxious gas eventually reached us, where we suffered with sore eyes and copious amounts of tears along with everyone else. We willingly joined fellow customers as they tried to fathom the cause of such a distressing incident. People had all manner of explanations as to what was causing this, from sliced onions, clogged drains and detergent, to burning rubbish, disinfectant and leaking stench pipes. After the air had cleared, we were all treated to a complementary meal. Now this was far more sophisticated behavior than the puerile schoolboy practice of deploying stink bombs.

Then came the big break. I had a call from the London Philharmonic Orchestra (LPO) asking if I was available to do some concerts for them as timpanist. I couldn't wait and felt very much at home behind the "tubs". Mostly. One of my first engagements was at Swansea's Brangwyn Hall where we were to do Beethoven's Piano Concerto #5, the "Emperor", which has a tricky duet with the piano at the end. It is always good to know what the soloist intends to do as they are a funny bunch and tend to play around with it at times. Sir Adrian did not like rehearsing one little bit and as we neared the end, put down his fishing rod and said, "You should be alright with this, Mr Cumberland". It was never considered a good idea to ask any conductor to rehearse anything, so it was something I had to live with. It was fine. One day at Abbey Road studios, he said at the beginning of the rehearsal to the amusement of the orchestra, "Good morning Cumbria". It was on the sad day in 1974 that the English counties of Cumberland and Westmorland became one (I still though have my sausages, pencils and of course The Gap). One very early experience was with Sir ACB (Adrian Cedric Boult) at Fairfield Halls, Croydon, where we were performing Wagner's *Wotan's Farewell* with the famous bass David Ward. Whilst the orchestra was playing the overture that had no timpani part, I was chatting over a bitter lemon in the bar with David who announced, "I'll be back shortly," and disappeared. I then heard a loud voice, "Timps you're on". I rushed to the stage where Sir Adrian had remained and as I was about to take my sticks for the opening roll he brought the baton down. As I scrambled to find a pair, the case was dislodged sending not only sticks but dampers, tuning keys, newspapers and other items to the floor. He looked over with a wry smile as if to say, "that'll teach you". It did. Despite this, playing the timps is what I really wanted to do! I was subsequently offered the principal job where I stayed for twenty years completely contented, travelling around the world many times.

This period with the LPO provided me with some of the most moving moments of my life. I still to this day get "goose bumps" when I think of Tennstedt's Mahler, Krips' Mozart, Haitink's Bruckner, Boult's Elgar, Giulini's Verdi and the joy of hearing Jessye Norman's *Four Last Songs,* Joan

Sutherland's *Turandot,* Domingo's "Rudolfo". Oistrakh's Tchaikovsky and the Brahms with Nathan Milstein. To experience Kempe's *Ein Heldenleben* (with the RPO), to be with Rostropovich when he played every cello concerto (with the LSO) in just two weeks and to work regularly with Barenboim, Pavarotti, Perahia, Perlman, Baker, Szeryng, Bachauer, Arrau, Rubinstein, Bernstein, Britten and to have also played for Copland, Stokowski, Richter, and so many, many more.

What more can a man want, but to be so happy with life and actually enjoy driving (*not* in a Volvo) to work every single day (*not* when Solti was on the box)?

Glyndebourne

A large and most enjoyable period of my life with the LPO was spent in Glyndebourne. Glyndebourne is a privately-owned opera house in Lewes, East Sussex, UK, set in hundreds of acres of beautiful countryside, with the annual festival running from May to August. The audience is expected to wear formal attire and the usual program for the day would involve arriving around 3pm and securing a place by one of the lakes to enjoy dinner. Butlers are common and limousines fill the car park (excepting the orchestral members' car park, which is out of sight). Helicopters were frequently seen and their passengers were equally keen to be seen. The drawback was that as they landed on the lawn, great clouds of dust were generated and the ladies' (and sometimes gentlemen's) costly hairdos were quickly transformed into birds' nests, toupees re-positioned and the beautiful dresses of these frightfully rich people were blown up over their heads. This practice was discontinued when a helicopter crashed into the trees after one performance. A glass or two of bubbly is the accepted refreshment of the day. The operas start around 5.15 with a long interval, around ninety minutes, for the audience to enjoy further glasses of champagne and fine wine in the perfect setting to experience their foie gras, lobsters, oysters, quail, smoked salmon, etc. whilst orchestral members adjourn to the pub for sausages, chips and a pint. In the second half of the performances, it was not unusual for arias to be accompanied by involuntary noises and loud snoring coming from the auditorium.

After the long interval of Verdi's *Falstaff,* it was found that one of the trombonists was not present. Despite several calls, he was nowhere to be found. The orchestral manager, John Cobb, who as luck would have it, also played the trombone, stood in for the missing person. An immediate search of the grounds was ordered by staff and after fifteen minutes or so, the nearest picturesque lake was found to contain not only stunning water lilies and small amphibians, but a member of the LPO. Complete in dinner suit and bow tie, the bedraggled musician was fished out by the ushers, taken to the wardrobe and in a new set of dry clothes preceded to the pit to resume service.

It was quite the norm for the timpani and trumpets, who almost always play the same parts in classical music, to leave the pit during the long tacets and (in Glyndebourne) play snooker or indulge in other activities, then upon hearing the cue from the speakers would return in good time to perform the next aria/chorus or whatever. There was never a problem in Glyndebourne as we would creep in at an appropriate time, albeit at the last moment. This turned out rather differently when we opened a new hall on London's South Bank, a place which was still in the final stages of construction. We took a production of one of the Mozart operas, works we knew so well, after the season and had a brief sound check before the performance with Bernard Haitink. As was the custom, the three of us left the pit for refreshment within earshot of the tannoy. With the cue coming up, we made our way back to the pit and tried to open the door. It was locked. The moment of our entry was coming up and we banged on the door. No response. With just a few bars to go we shouted and kicked but to no avail. We could all anticipate Bernard's face when he would look over to give us the cue. We were unable to get in and totally missed it. We eventually found our way around the side of the hall into a back entrance and slinked into position and stayed there, even in long tacet numbers until the end, not daring to have eye contact with "the stick".

The principal trumpet player at the time was Laurence Evans from deep in the valleys of Wales. No reference to Glyndebourne in this book would be complete without mention of Laurie and his unique contribution to the LPO with his stunning Mahler 5s amongst other works and the occasional sleeping periods instead of playing. Despite this, Laurie took his trumpet playing very seriously and I can never remember him ever falling off a note. Away from the platform though, he did like to let his hair down from time to time every day. For the long season at Glyndebourne every year we all needed to find accommodation and he had found a new cottage conveniently situated just a stone's throw from the "Trevor Arms", a licensed establishment. After a rehearsal at the opera house one Sunday, we adjourned to the Trevor for a much-needed beverage when Laurie, who admitted to being absent-minded at times, announced that he would pop back to the cottage to check on the progress of the chicken which he had put on during the morning break. He came back trembling some short while later looking even more confused and disheveled than normal, announcing that he had thought it strange that in the kitchen, the strong smell was something other than that of a roasting bird. He had wandered over to the electric stove and, not realizing quite where he had gone wrong, lit a match. The resultant deafening explosion caused the oven door to fly open and propel the cold chicken with some considerable force into the wall, breaking every bone in its body.

Something quite different happened when many trumpet players from the London orchestras gathered in a public house in Covent Garden to celebrate a colleague's birthday. These occasions were generally (always) associated with committed drinking but for some inexplicable reason, Laurie was then "on the wagon". Towards the latter part of the evening, word got around that Mr Plod was sitting with a colleague in a police car just out of sight of the pub doors. The boys came up with a cunning plan. At closing time, Laurie walked very unsteadily towards his red Morgan and fumbled around in his pockets to find the keys. Whilst doing this, the other lads slipped away quietly to find their own cars and drive away without incident. Laurie got the thing going and drove a few metres down the road before being pulled over and breathalyzed to record a reading of 00.00.

Bernard did however see the funny side of some things in the pit at Glyndebourne, when after a few minutes of the start of a Richard Strauss opera one evening, there was a total blackout. Nobody could see a thing except for a white tuxedo searching for the panic button behind the podium, the phone and the red/green cue lights which had gone out. Above the music, he shouted inaudible messages to the stage crew who were frantically trying to sort things out. At this time he stopped conducting, expecting the playing of this complex score to collapse, but it didn't as the orchestra continued to play quite normally until light was restored some thirty seconds later. He couldn't believe it.

In one performance, he was somewhat shocked to see a full breasted person with beautiful flowing blonde hair enter the pit and play the triangle before vanishing. Then came another person in armour with a dagger through his skull. Still recovering from that experience, a donkey appeared at the back to play the bass drum before trotting off. My colleagues had of course wandered into the wardrobe to procure these items. BH simply did not know what was coming next.

As was, or *is*, my wont, I decided to be a little out of the ordinary in the final performance of Richard Strauss' *Ariadne auf Naxos*. At the beginning of Act 2, I have around forty minutes of tacet after which I play a single short *ff* D at the very end of Zerbinetta's famous aria. I thought it would be nice to do something different that night. It turned out to be not so funny but an

30

almost life threatening situation for the conductor Aldo Ceccato, who is Italian. At the end of the interval and before embarking on a snooker match with my colleagues, I entered the pit, pre-tuned my timp to the required D and took a stick from the case. Procuring some string from the wardrobe department I tied it to the end of the cue. I planned not to enter the pit at the usual climax at the end of the aria but to leave the door ajar with just enough room to slide the cue/stick inside. I was watching and could see Ceccato's anxiety and look of despair as I was not there. Mamma Mia! He panicked because he is Italian. At the last moment I brought the then unseen cue/stick up and struck the drum at the right moment, or so I thought. Had I taken my physics lessons at school more seriously, I would have remembered that when bringing a ball of felt attached to a long rod vertically from ground level to about a metre above the timpani and down again onto the head takes significantly more time than a direct stroke from the wrist. It was late. Another oversight was that the instrument generally does not damp itself, so it rang on. My immediate colleagues did find it extremely funny but Aldo didn't, because he is Italian.

It was with our beloved John Pritchard when something extremely naughty happened. As well as conducting, John played the continuo himself in the Mozarts and such was his brilliant mind, he often weaved a few bars of a recitative from a different opera into that which we were doing and would always glance around to see who had noticed. It was on the last night of one of them that during the interval someone had inserted a large uncooked pork sausage into his score. When seeing the thing, he picked it up and promptly used it as a baton. Knowing John's persuasions, we all knew he was secretly hoping he could soon "bring it to life".

My travels

We travelled extensively and following are a few examples of what could (and did) go wrong.

Russia

My first trip overseas was when I was thirteen with the National Youth Orchestra. We were transported in a Hermes propeller aircraft which wasn't very nice. The trip included Hamburg, Stockholm and Russia amongst other countries, quite an experience for one so young. Russia was awful. We had the feeling of being watched the whole time. The food was totally unacceptable resulting in a constant diarrheal condition which wasn't made any easier with the toilet tissue manufactured in crepe paper. Blood was involved on a daily basis and I couldn't wait to get out of the place and vowed never to return. With my involvement in the National Theatre, we were invited to visit Canada, which was wonderful, starting in Vancouver and finishing in Toronto, and would you believe Russia? Common sense prevailed and I agreed to travel. After all, I didn't really have a deputy. We were all invited to the Russian embassy in Kensington where I had my first gin and tonic. We were accommodated in the very same hotel as we were with the NYO and again treated royally. The cast was given priority to enter the mausoleum to view both Lenin and Stalin before they were separated. The shows were generally without incident in the Kremlevsky Theatre in Red Square but for one unforgettable night. It was Congreve's restoration comedy, *Love for Love,* and the show featured us four musicians singing a harmonised "Te aeternum Patrem omnis terra venerator" (in falsetto of course). Before each show, we had to go to our dressing rooms where the dresser would cut strands of our own hair to stick to the bald wig which was glued to our heads so as to resemble street musicians suffering from scurvy. After the show, the rubbery items were removed and a large quantity of sweat was poured down the sink. We soon had this ritual removed. One night, the show was running smoothly as we waited for our cue for a solo vocal item (with the unlikely ensemble of Eb clarinet, D trumpet, cello and glockenspiel) of "and I see one who can sing it". The musician involved was the as yet unknown young boy actor Leonard Whiting, who went on to famously portray Romeo with Olivia Hussey in Zefferelli's film of Shakespeare's *Romeo and Juliet.* When we heard the cue, Leonard was nowhere to be seen. The cue was repeated in a rather more anxious and at a greater dynamic, *"and I can see one who can (bloody well) sing it"*. We four were kind of capable but were not familiar enough with the words. The actors were all ad-libbing for some minutes. Leonard, having suffered the experience of an anal collapse as the solids in his stomach became liquids, rushed to the stage completely out of breath and went down on his knees panting. Not a sound came out. So it was just the accompaniment for the first verse until he regained composure to huskily make it to the end. The decision was made there and then to definitely never return. In my initial year with the LPO, the first overseas tour was to Russia to work with Shostakovich senior. Can you believe it? I did not go. Idiot!

Israel
Whilst with the London Mozart Players, I was asked to go to Israel to play *Les Noces* with Stravinsky. I was young and learning about life as Sidney Sax, the well-known "fixer" in London had asked me to do a string of film sessions, which in those days were quite lucrative (he always phoned and

said, in Jewish tones, "Alan, I need your sound from 13 to 17 January". Quite naturally I accepted the sessions and gave the timp job away. Again — idiot!

USA

This was my first opportunity to cross the pond. Jimmy Holland asked me to go with the LSO to Daytona Beach, Florida, for the inaugural concert of the festival, which has been running ever since. It was a unique experience for me in that I had never at that stage been in such a climate to enjoy the lavish attention from our wonderful hosts. I was the youngest member of the LSO at that time and was overwhelmed by things that were offered to us all. Midnight golf (after having been compulsorily smothered in insect repellant), being driven around the steeply banked Daytona race track at high speed, deep sea fishing where I, with considerable help from our fishermen, hooked and brought in a 40lb amberjack, water skiing which, after a lesson on the beach, I managed to rise successfully causing the boat personnel to shout, "You've done this before". My reply was, "I have not," before they steered the boat into a ninety degree turn causing me to cross the fast running wash resulting in a dump into the sea where I have to say I floundered helplessly. I had great difficulty in re-attaching the skis to my feet. It was useless and the only way out was to be assisted to clamber back into the boat. This was not easy. Sunburn was also an issue here with having to squeeze water blisters from my face on a regular basis. Teeth created yet another problem in that my already aching fangs became infected and all my wisdom teeth had to be removed in one go. I was given gas to put me out but when coming around and leaving the chair, I fainted for the first and only time in my life (so far). But the show had to go on and I was there in the Peabody auditorium that night to play the last note of Bliss's *A Colour Symphony* upon the cymbals.

The thirtieth of July, 1966, was a date that shall remain indelible in my mind. The World Cup final between England and West Germany. Colin Davis was more than happy to cancel the rehearsal so he could join the rest of the orchestra in watching the event. We settled down just before 10am to watch the live coverage from Wembley with the kick off at 3pm. I was sat next to my colleague, the principal timpanist of the LSO, Kurt-Hans Goedicke. I was English and he was German. We all enjoyed a thrilling match which involved extra time. Sadly, I cannot remember the final result. We were invited to a cook-out nearly every night at various venues which were hosted by some generous and beautiful people. I returned for the second year to receive yet more hospitality. What a life! All too much for me! My thoughts went back to the office at Eastern Electricity Board in Luton.

One trip did not turn out so well. With the LPO we played in several cities and were given a much needed free day in Denver, Colorado—just the concert in the evening. My best friend, John Cobb, who was the orchestral manager, and I decided to go snow skiing this time. I had been a few times in Europe, always taking my winter break with Neil Levesley, the principal bassoonist. Strangely, this somehow always seemed to coincide with Solti's two-week annual stint with the orchestra. I went through the basics with John, teaching him how to turn around without allowing one ski to cross over and pin the other to the ground, and how to stop in a "snow plough" position etc. It was not long before we were out on the nursery slopes getting the feel of things. I then suggested that we take the chair lift to the intermediate station where we would alight and ski gently down first time. We boarded successfully and apart from being terrified swaying around high above the mountain were seemingly calm and collected. As we approached the station, I recommended that John should jump off to the left and me to the right. If he started sliding away I told him to fall over and wait for me. We certainly were not prepared for what happened next. John's bindings on his right boot and my left one somehow managed to become intertwined so we both had to jump off together to the left. I fell first and John, the heavier man, had no option but to fall on top of me which he did with a sickening thump on my right leg. The boots were disentangled and we sat for a while. I broke out in a strange cold sweat. At this stage the foot wasn't hurting too much so we stood up. I then suggested that we ski down slowly and I would go on later and wait at the bottom. There was no problem going down and I was really enjoying myself despite travelling at a speed over which I had little control. At the turn around place I did the traditional snow spray stop by angling both legs to the side, at which point there was a worrying crack from my right ankle. I waited for John and decided to take the boot off. It wouldn't budge. I needed a paramedic who was on hand to help and it was finally removed revealing a heavily swollen foot.

I was taken to the hospital where it was revealed that I had broken my posterior malleolus (which I am told is pretty well impossible to break). This caused me to be placed in a plaster cast which went from toe to groin. I asked the doctors to put a soft bandage on the leg, but they said they could not—it had to be hard and I must stay in hospital that night. This caused some concern because we were doing Mahler 5 (we always did Mahler 5 everywhere we went) a few hours later. The pedaling especially at the end definitely requires two feet. If only I could get out of that cast. My dear friend Keith Millar, the principal percussionist, who had a knack of getting people out of difficult situations (he had done it so many times) was called and he arrived at the hospital to tell the doctors they had no choice but to let me go. Reluctantly they did and gave me a wheelchair to the concert hall.

I was in light blue hospital pyjamas and was given crutches and a walking stick. My concert wear was brought from the hotel and the tail coat and shirt were no problem, but of course, I couldn't wear the trousers. So there I was with a tail top, shirt and bow tie and a cummerbund around the top of my pyjamas. People for some reason found the whole situation very funny. One thoughtful viola player, Judy Swan, brought me her black undergarment which I put on, so all appeared as normal. The orchestra went onto the stage and the brass players walked in front of me hobbling along so that the audience couldn't see me. I was helped onto my high timpani stool and positioned myself with the rigid right leg out to the side of my smallest drum. It felt distinctly awkward, but then, as I was playing, the slip, which happened to be made of nylon started to slide and I was going down (I now know why it is called a slip). I had no support from the right foot and playing with just one hand (which is tricky when rolling) and a left foot to prevent me falling to the floor. As hard as I tried to stay put, I was on the move. I had no choice but to stop playing to avoid headlines in the next day's press and somehow got through the whole program with only my left foot. It may sound strange but when your right leg is out so far to the right and pedaling is required on the lower drums, the groin area becomes tight and distinctly uncomfortable.

The next day we had an evening off and decided to dine at the famous Ruth's Chris, a high class steak house full of well-heeled people. I was with all my percussion colleagues and we were placed at a table in the middle of the restaurant. My crutches were put in the corner by the waiter. It turned out to be a long evening and several bottles of fine wine were consumed, in my case, to ease the pain. Sorting out the bill, Keith, who as previously mentioned was used to getting people out of difficult situations, soon found out that the tables were about to turn, which they did. He thoughtfully walked, albeit unsteadily, to retrieve my crutches and decided to use them to get back to the table. This was an exciting new experience for him but sadly things went horribly wrong. Trying to balance whilst looking dignified, he fell backwards into the middle of a table of stunned diners. Unfortunately, the tables were round and hinged in the middle for easy stacking. He fell right into the crack causing both sides of the table to rise sharply sending steaks and wine everywhere. Although some ladies were not amused, everybody seemed to appreciate it was just an unfortunate accident. As far as

I can recall, the patrons were treated to another meal. We then caught a taxi back to the hotel and on the journey realised that Keith was no longer with us. At last sight he was sitting in the front bench seat of the cab but had quietly slithered onto the floor beside the driver. The evening ended with us putting him to bed rather than the other way round.

Interestingly, upon returning to the UK, my first stop was to visit the hospital where they removed the plaster, took x-rays and confirmed that it *was* the posterior malleolus that was broken, never before encountered in that hospital. The plaster was replaced with a cast from the knee down which was much more comfortable. Driving then became an issue. John Cobb swapped his automatic Mitsubishi with my manual Nissan and we were ready to go. With my previous automatics, I always used right foot accelerator and left foot brake, a technique which I use to this day. Lucky I use my feet in my job! But this was different as I had only a left foot at my disposal. It was not difficult to left foot everything, but there was nowhere for the right one to go. As mentioned, it was a lower leg plaster which meant I could bend the leg and prop the foot underneath my left knee. Problem solved.

Another unusual incident occurred in US, which should not go unmentioned. We were playing at a prominent university with the usual program of an overture, concerto and Mahler (5). At the interval, the orchestra was required to walk from the stage through a large utility room through to the refreshment area. Upon entering this place, we noticed several members of the Mahler orchestra had gathered to witness something quite out of the ordinary. Klaus was with us and could scarcely believe his eyes when he saw a prominent member of the orchestra, in tails, spinning around in an industrial dryer (the electricity was not switched on, so a helping hand had been given to start the revolutions). Klaus' mouth opened wide, his eyes popped and he needed support from a nearby table as his legs wobbled even more than when he was on the box. He tried to gather his composure and imagine this was all only a silly dream. We were greatly relieved when the movement stopped so the poor man could be released. Alas, the door would not open despite much banging on the thickened glass. Our friend was looking none too happy. Then the much-welcomed click from the door and it opened. Out he came in a state of daze and bewilderment. Klaus Tennstedt quickly summoned enough strength to shuffle away and receive his much-needed Carlsberg Special (followed by another couple no doubt). During the symphony, he frequently glanced up to the back to see if this pale-faced member of his orchestra was still able to play. The following day, we were on a plane going to the next city when we heard an announcement asking if there was a doctor on board. A smart looking man came down from the front to look at the person sitting behind me. It was our adventurous colleague. Some sedation was administered and as we landed, a team of paramedics was on hand to receive the passenger. Keith M was by his side all the time (again) and was asked on the way to the hospital if the patient had done anything unusual in the last twenty-four hours. Keith replied, "No, not at all as far as I know, except for spinning around in a commercial tumble dryer".

Mexico

Here, we were all, especially the wind players, concerned about our breathing at such a height above sea level. My perc colleagues and I decided to climb a huge flight of steps to a monument. This was achieved at sloth like speed with pulmonary discomfort. As usual, we were always ready to sample the local fare and returned without too much difficulty to the bottom to enjoy some chilli con carne, the hottest food I had ever experienced. Several beers were needed to aid the process of digestion. After the meal, we visited the adjacent men's facility to relieve ourselves where we were joined by a largish local gentleman who it transpired was suffering with severe flatulence. Standing at the urinal with arms akimbo and legs apart, the performance began with an accented Bb in **mp**. A *crescendo* soon followed as the air pressure dramatically increased and despite intense vibrations and occasional sphinctoral flapping, the well supported sound developed into one of sonority and depth. The pitch, phrasing and wide-ranging dynamics were determined entirely by convulsions. Dyspepsia was temporarily relieved by the quick release of some relatively minor pockets of air prior to some powerful belching, which did the trick. He was in full flow. We could only admire his use of the advanced technique of circular anal breathing as the recital continued relentlessly before coming to an abrupt end when we feared for a moment that he may have "followed through". As soon as it had stopped it started again with a series of fast staccato *ff* pops which coincided with the sharp movements of his right hand. These quickly lost momentum and petered out bringing this well rounded, musically shaped performance to a close, ending as it started in **mp** as the last drops were shaken from his appendage. He zipped himself up and walked away totally satisfied as though this was the norm.

Far East

It was with the LPO that I had my first taste of the Far East with a tour of Hong Kong, Singapore, South Korea and Japan. There were several interesting things to recall with this new experience.

The landing at Kai Tak airport in Hong Kong was quite extraordinary in that the planes came in so close to the buildings, you could see the entire components of the residents' meals (rice) from the window. Then the very sharp right-hand turn before the rapid final descent which had to be spot-on if an extension of the flight as a sea plane in the South China Sea was to be avoided. We stayed in the Hong Kong hotel, which was on the other side of the harbour where we were to perform in the Hong Kong City Hall, a rather small venue but with an acceptable acoustic. I suppose it was good in some ways as we had to travel on the infamous Star Ferry, but it became tedious day after day. Now, the Hong Kong Philharmonic Orchestra (HKPO) and international orchestras perform in a monstrosity on Kowloon side—the Hong Kong Cultural Centre, an eyesore that stands directly on the waterfront in the middle of Tsim Sha Tsui, overlooking one of the world's most photographed vistas. This building, unbelievably, has no windows, no restaurant and no bar, so local and international concert goers and visitors are unable to have a meal, a drink or view beautiful Hong Kong island before their concert in an acoustically poor environment. How anybody can design a hideous building like that is beyond my comprehension and who on earth gives it council approval to go ahead? Hopefully the right people will be consulted before the construction starts on a new arts centre in west Kowloon. As we looked at the audience in this part of the world, it was the black hair that struck us. Everybody. We were so used to different shades of hair, including white, brown, blonde and much blue, especially in Eastbourne. Singapore was interesting with the ladymen in Bugis Street, but little else apart from the zoo to interest us, and Korea with "ladies of the night" filling the lobbies of our hotel by day as well. In Seoul we were given a sumptuous buffet lunch comprising mainly traditional Korean food. Shortly before the concert, almost the entire orchestra complained of severe stomach discomfort and became desperate when told that all the toilets in the back stage area of the concert hall were blocked, save that in the conductor's room. Complementary clothes pegs for our noses were not provided. Sadly we were also unable to find a stall that sold corks. Japan was as we anticipated, with everything precisely organized and timed to perfection. On one occasion when we were travelling by Shinkansen, the bullet train, the rather aloof principal viola player, Quintin Ballardie, OBE, FRAM, decided to get off at a stop to buy coffee or something. He was told to hurry, and in his familiar style took no notice. Those trains wait for no man. It was with some satisfaction that we waved him a fond goodbye as the train moved off. Shinjuku was filled on a daily basis with business men plying themselves with Suntory whisky after a hard day at the office making lots of money but our job was to make music which we enjoyed in Bunka Kaikan hall.

After the always satisfying but totally draining emotional experience of the evening's performance (Mahler 5) it was the tradition to retire and enjoy a "nightcap" in one of our rooms. In each suite, there was invariably an electric trouser press which one night proved too much of a temptation for our principal percussionist to resist. Always dapper, he decided his trousers needed pressing for presentation the following morning, but wasn't game enough to remove them before inserting them in the machine. He climbed in fully clothed and found a reasonably comfortable position, but as the boys were pressing the levers to flatten him and his trousers, the whole thing snapped in half with him and broken pieces of the device falling to the floor. He wasn't unduly perturbed as this situation was not uncommon on tour.

Another strange thing happened one night in Tokyo when I joined my close colleague and friend, Peter Chrippes, in his room for the "last of the day". As we were enjoying the nectar, his wife phoned from England so I left him to it and took my drink to the end of the corridor and opened one of those doors with a horizontal bar that required pushing hard. It shut behind me. Out I went and found myself on the balcony on an extremely high floor. I was not good at heights and decided to go straight back inside. Unfortunately, these doors do not open from the outside. Very soon searchlights were directed right at me and a rescue vehicle was in place some fifty or so floors beneath. There were shouts in animated English from the loud speakers, *"do not jump, we weir lescue you"*. All I had was a gin and tonic in my hand which I did not really want to waste. In no time the security crew opened the door from the inside, grabbed me Japanese style and hauled me in, glass and contents intact. They realized it was a simple mistake and were very nice about the whole episode, although privately probably sorry that there wasn't a more dramatic ending.

We returned to these countries on a regular basis without major incident and the usual excellent performances with John Pritchard, Bernard Haitink, Klaus Tennstedt and others. It was on one of our frequent journeys to the East that another hilarious event occurred. After the usual preflight gathering of the percs in the bar at Heathrow, we wandered through to the boarding lounge at terminal three, where, amongst a hundred or so members of the orchestra, were two mature, gaunt gentlemen sitting bolt upright next to each other as if conjoined. They were staring straight ahead saying nothing. It was immediately apparent that their hair was not entirely natural as they sported striking hairpieces, one in mandarin orange and the other canary yellow. They were both supported by a flat cap. As hard as it was not to look, we found it impossible. Upon assuming our designated seats at the back of the aircraft, there, in the two seats behind the bulkhead were the same two persons, still wearing their caps. The gentleman with the vibrant yellow piece was sitting by the window. After the usual cocktails and free-flowing complimentary alcoholic drinks with the meal, we sensed something was afoot. The atmosphere was not normal. Our colleague, a highly respected principal player in London and the same person who was spun-dried on a previous tour had somehow acquired a long length of thread from the cabin crew. He carefully fashioned a slip knot at one end, then, leaving the remaining thread in his seat some four rows back, walked to the front to temporarily swap seats with another LPO member who was positioned directly behind the passenger with the lemon hair. Whilst in a crouching position, he attached the knot to the little button in the middle of the cap and secured it as tightly as he dared. It was not too difficult, as the cap and horse hair, or whatever it was, were between that and the scalp. Both men remained motionless. Original seats were resumed and all was calm for a while, but it was soon to change. We all knew what was about to happen. Suddenly, with a deft flick of the wrist, the cap was whisked from his head towards the back, causing the yellow thatch to turn ninety degrees and the men to simultaneously grab their heads with both hands, in the same way footballers do when they've missed a penalty, and assume the BRACE, BRACE position. After a few minutes, and with the rug having been surreptitiously re-aligned, they rose together, when the more unfortunate of the two turned around and said *"ez enyvun zeen my et?"* The whole compartment of the plane was in pain as the two men tentatively reclined into a more comfortable position. Sometime later, a member of the orchestra walked forward and said, "is this yours, sir?" They both spent the remainder of the journey rather lower in their seats than before, with just the one hand securing their headwear, for fear something even more dreadful was to befall them.

China

This momentous trip happened in 1973 when the LPO, the first orchestra ever from the west was invited to the principal cities of mainland China. No one knew what to expect. All we knew is that JP was the conductor, a terrific friend of the orchestra and brilliant musician, Ida Haendel the soloist with the Elgar, a Chinese encore at the ready and our usual programs. It was preceded by a week in Hong Kong. We were taken by a rickety train to Guangzhou, just inside the Chinese border where we were met by many officials from the government. This was a big moment. A lavish banquet was laid out before us in the large hall at the train station. We then realised that we must quickly adapt to the rather different culture in accepting that even at the highest diplomatic and cultural level, it was quite acceptable to do things up with which we were not brought. At each banquet (every day) we were sat one Chinese, one LPO, one Chinese, one LPO etc. The place was thick with cigarette smoke. We were relieved to be asked to stand every few minutes to drink a toast to each other. This involved a kind of prune juice in one glass and Mao Tai, the dreaded Chinese rice wine with a hugely powerful kick in the other. We were served delicacies such as chickens' feet, fishes' stomachs, snake, ox intestines and other delectable items, all with people smoking, coughing their guts up and accurately shooting phlegm projectiles into the spittoons under the table. Canton and Peking, as they were then, and Shanghai all featured. We were introduced to our air crew at Guangzhou who were to remain with us for the whole trip. The plane took off and climbed alarmingly to a not great height where it remained until it descended rapidly without the usual levelling off until it landed. No other planes seemed to be in the sky. With tea the preferred beverage, no alcohol was offered. Three coaches were provided for the orchestra and several limos for JP, management and Chinese officials. Thousands of people had lined the streets to welcome us and all traffic signals had been turned to green and other vehicles prohibited so we had a swift journey with a huge police escort to our destination. Upon our arrival, we were given RMB, the local currency, cigarettes and beer if we needed them (as per the norm, some viola players who neither smoked nor drunk alcohol readily accepted the gifts). At every free moment, we were taken by bus to the places we should see—the great wall, Forbidden City and many other interesting places including a trip down the Yangtze River past the warships (which we were not allowed to photograph).

The concerts were a huge success and the whole experience was overwhelming. There is one unusual incident that I should mention. It was in Shanghai, perhaps the most developed city we saw. We were well used to having people stare at us at every move, as they had never seen people with colourful clothes (everyone in China was dressed in black, grey or dark blue) or indeed different colour hair, in my case auburn. Everywhere we went, people stopped and ogled in disbelief. At concert time, we went for the usual light meal and a beer. Upon our return to the concert hall, we were told the toilets were in the public area at the front of the building where the audience had assembled. The men's toilets were jammed full of people, but we had to "go" so as not to disgrace ourselves on stage. When the public saw us enter the urinal, the crowd spread inviting my colleagues and I to go first. Standing there preparing to open the flies was embarrassing to say the least as the crowd had gathered around to look closely and see if we "were made the same". As any man will tell you, it is not only difficult, but impossible to proceed under this pressure but was essential to relieve ourselves. With enormous will power and inner bladder strength we held on until the interval where we found a female toilet a short distance away. The whole journey was a massive eye-opener and a fantastic experience.

Thailand

After giving masterclasses in Melbourne, I was invited for a Thai meal with my colleagues from the Victorian College of the Arts and enjoyed a couple of pre-prandial drinks. After a few sips of Tom Yum Goong I felt beads of sweat upon my brow and simply thought it was the spiciness of the soup that was affecting me in an unusual way. I ordered another beer to cool me down and quickly found I could neither eat nor drink any more. There was a strong reaction to something. My tongue and palms swelled up alarmingly and I had to be taken to the hospital to recover. I was told it was simply an allergy, then undetermined, from which I mercifully recovered overnight.

It was with my students from Queensland that I first visited Bangkok when we had a lengthy stopover. Upon our return, Tania Savage and I were subjected to an "in-depth" search at the airport. Quite what the customs officers were looking for we don't know, but it kept our families waiting for ever. Whilst in Brisbane, I was contacted by the orchestral manager of the LSO, John Duffy, to ask if I would be the timpanist for the World Philharmonic Orchestra to play Mahler 1 in Bangkok for the anniversary of King Bhumibol, the much revered King of Thailand. This was an opportunity at which I jumped and had the chance to meet up with many old mates from the LSO, including Malcolm Hall, Rod Franks and the legendary Maurice Murphy, as well as many from Australian orchestras. It was quite an occasion. After the show, I was treated to a local Thai Singha beer. At the first sip, my lips became numb, just the same feeling as at the restaurant in Melbourne. I immediately knew it was the beer and not the food that was affecting me. This was later confirmed by an allergist in Brisbane who found the culprit to be the addition of formaldehyde in its recipe. Ladymen also feature quite prominently in Thailand and I have been with different guests to see their popular show three times. These days, at the end of the performance, the beautiful creatures expose their breasts, which is rather nice. When returning from one show to the Sheraton Orchid hotel which overlooks the Chao Phraya river, Tony Bedewi, Han Ying and I enjoyed a lobster pizza at midnight on the rooftop whilst watching a truly magnificent firework display. I asked the waiter what the occasion was, and he answered, *"It's for you, sir!"*

I have returned to Bangkok on an annual basis either with my work or simply for holidays where we are entertained royally with authentic Thai food by my former students, including Chanannat, Komsun, Lertkiat, Siripong, Salina, Apachai and many, many more. Sadly, the last two visits to adjudicate at the Thai Young Musician of the Year were affected by the shocking floods and the "red shirts" riots, when we were locked in our hotel for some days. This was made all the worse as I was unable to have more clothes made.

Europe
The LPO visited Spain many times and we became friends of the restaurateurs who worked in Los Caracoles, the famous tapas bar and restaurant in Barcelona. No trip to Spain would be complete without a visit. On the first day we headed at lunchtime straight down La Rambla for the restaurant and enjoyed a suckling pig and a few glasses. Back for the siesta and then to the concert hall for a sound test. Back to the hotel for another rest, as the concerts there start so late, and then on to the concert after which we caught a cab back to the same restaurant. The suckling pig was so good at lunch time, that after my garlic prawns I foolishly decided to order another one. Exquisite. It was only back at the hotel I felt a little queasy. I had consumed large quantities of fat and crackling during the day and it wanted to come out. It did and I shot the proverbial cat down the toilet (one of my former students and dear friends, David Arnold, had a pet cat and called it "Shot").

Italy
I recall one night in Rome where we were performing at the Coliseum. We had completed the customary sound check at around 5, then went for a bite to eat. Upon returning to check everything shortly before the concert later that evening, I was horrified to find that it had been raining, or so I thought. My heads were covered in a film of water which was dripping down the bowls. Nowhere else seemed to be wet. It was the humidity. So I wiped it off and all seemed well. The only work on the program was Beethoven Symphony 9, televised. All began well, but halfway down the second page

strange things started to happen. Was it Beethoven warning me not to change the Ds to Gs four bars before the last *Allegro ma non tanto* in the last movement? My arms and wrists seemed to be tiring. There was precious little sound coming from the drums. A spiraling (and I'm sure welcoming) spray was showering the trumpets creating a magnificent rainbow between me and the TV lights. Very pretty. What was going on? It was all created by increasing water on the heads which was picked up by the rolling sticks causing this phenomenon. This was a first for me. The sticks felt like used dish mops, or more precisely *floor* mops on this occasion and I went through several pairs that night. Boy, was I tired. Why did it have to be Beethoven 9? I suppose I should be thankful it wasn't Bruckner or Sibelius.

In 1982, the orchestra celebrated its golden anniversary and undertook a massive tour (with the dreaded conducting monkey) which included many countries—one each day. Now that sounds glamorous, but all we see on trips like this are planes, coaches, hotels and concert halls. We were given a wad of notes each day for our subsistence (this is before the Euro) and ended up with pockets full of roubles, deutschmarks, francs, pesos, lira and florints to name but a few, but it was the hotels that were the most fun. It was impossible to remember your room number as keys were given rather than the plastic cards these days. To turn the lights and TV on and off was not always as easy as it might appear, but the shower! Every one was different. Do you pull the lever out or move it sideways? How do you control the temperature? How do you ensure the water doesn't come from the top and freeze or scald you?

Whilst overlooking the aircraft in the departure lounge at Barcelona airport in a ferocious storm, a witty member of the orchestra said, "the rain in Spain falls mainly on the plane". The be-Homburged GS was often seen with his wife alone on the bendy buses that used to ferry the passengers to the aircraft. He did not like to travel with us lesser mortals. But it was most generous of him to throw a party for the orchestra after our last concert where we were rationed to one alcoholic drink. He gave a short speech which included the line, "Thank you all for your hard work on this grueling tour. You did very well but it wasn't quite as good as my boys in Chicago". What an insult. He wasn't very good either. We all left.

Australia

This trip in 1985 was memorable for other reasons. Our tour was scheduled just three months after breaking my leg in America. As it was the hottest I had ever been (43) we went on our first day to Cottesloe beach for a swim. We were a little wary of box jellyfish and sharks but certainly not of surges in the current. There were many signs warning of dangerous "rips" in the sea. Being English, we took no notice. What's a little rip? Soon after entering the water, I could feel the strength of an underwater current trying to remove my trunks and break my neck but suddenly the power was so strong it turned me upside down causing me to ingest large quantities of water and hit my head on the sand at the bottom. This twisted my still bad foot and I was in more pain for some days. But to take my mind away from this, our first performance was the next day at the opening of the Leeuwin Estate Winery, some four hours away from Perth. It was really hot and arriving at the hall, the string players quite understandably refused to open their cases so their instruments had a chance to become acclimatised to the extremes of temperature. With an utterly useless conductor, Avi Ostrowski (the last-minute replacement for Yevgeni Svetlanov, who had an unfortunate accident in a Russian hospital where an endoscopic instrument had exploded inside his chest), a well-known program, and an outdoor concert in a winery, a rehearsal was not high on the list of priorities. It was with relief then, that this was cancelled and a guided tour of the establishment was hastily arranged. As one would expect, each wine should be sampled, and they were—all of them. Spittoons were not required on this occasion. Come the concert, not every member of the orchestra was entirely sober if I was truthful and some were not sober at all. The televised concert started well, complete with cicadas which constantly dive-bombed the reflective heads of the timpani to which they were attracted. It occurred to me though, in tacet passages, with my arms folded, if I kept the pedals at the lowest note of the range, that upon impact from the buzzing insects, I could surreptitiously whack them up to the top note without anybody seeing what I was doing creating a loud, ascending "doyng, doyng" sound. The concert, complete with other unfamiliar creatures in the audience, toads, plovers and other calling birds, hysterical kookaburras in particular, went off without further incident (as far as I remember). Afterwards we were invited to a reception the like of which I had never seen. Wine glasses were hung around our necks and constantly replenished. The array of thousands of magnificent crabs, prawns, lobsters and the like had to be seen to be believed. Magnificent. The coaches left around 1am and several cases of the wine were placed in the aisle for all to consume. This was done, and with the combination of jet lag had an effect on some. So then off to Melbourne, Sydney, and the opening of the Queensland Performing Arts Complex (QPAC) in Brisbane was to follow. The Australians again treated us royally and the reception that followed our concert was out on the balcony of the hall when a whole animal was spit-roasted for us. Yet more lovely Australian wine was stacked up in vast quantities. I fell in love with the people and the country and upon invitation moved to Brisbane in 1987 where I spent eleven glorious years before moving on to Hong Kong.

My relocation to Brisbane with my family should have been relatively straightforward, but wasn't, as English is not spoken in that country. As Sir Laurence Olivier said, "there are five things wrong with the Australian language—the vowels". He was right and my two daughters often returned crying from school announcing that they could not understand what the teachers were saying. We all soon picked up the brogue, talked like Ockers and everything was fine. The then percussion department of the conservatorium was not in good shape, so it was my job to fix it. I had some talented players who I wanted to look after. There were around ten students each year. I soon formed a percussion ensemble that mainly specialised in classical music and we were soon performing in small concerts around the Brisbane area. With the arrival of the new Dean and Provost of the Qld Conservatorium, Anthony Camden, an overseas tour was arranged with my group. We discussed it over an Indian curry, to which my students had never been subjected. Wow! We were to go to the Philippines and meet up with a girls' choir where we gave some concerts. They were young and I must say not unattractive. We all had hosts and I was put with the director of the choir who was unfortunately a little more mature than her choristers. In fact very much more mature. Then we were off to the UK with concerts at the Aberdeen International Youth Festival in Scotland and in various places around the south of England. This was so successful that the next tour was already being planned. This was all done with the help of Anthony and the registrar of the "Con", John Hucks. When I met John on my first day there he was seated in his office drinking a mug of coffee. All seemed perfectly normal. As he stood up to greet me, his head touched the roof of the building. I hadn't realised that his mug was twice the normal size, as was he. I stepped well back to converse reducing the angle of refraction. He was exactly seven feet tall and used to play for the South African basketball team. He needed to arrange aisle seating on the plane and two beds in his accommodation. Low roofs in shopping malls and hotels were of concern. One of my students asked him once, "John, is everything in your body in proportion?" He said, "No. If it was I would be eight feet tall!"

To raise funds for the tour, we had to work hard and perform many concerts around the region, mainly for kids and "wrinklies". To ferry the instruments around, I had to acquire an HGV license, which I did, and transported them, with the students in the back of the truck, to and from the different venues. This wasn't entirely legal, but it was fun.

On the first overseas trip for one, Brett Carvolth, who was so desperate to have his first pint of Guinness, that soon after arriving I took him with others to the *Hole in the Wall*, a watering establishment underneath the arches at Waterloo station, adjacent to the Royal Festival Hall (this was directly after our eight hour flight from Brisbane, a four hour stopover in Singapore and then a fourteen hour leg to Heathrow). For the first few minutes he was in heaven but then rapidly became "loose" and folded on the table after a half pint or so. First time to see someone fall asleep over a pint of Guinness. He more than made up for it the following day. Later into the tour, I introduced them to Atlantic prawns, with which they fell in love (as well as the Philippinos), Scottish salmon, real ale and many other Pommie delights.

We were all so excited. After this I made it compulsory for my students to compose or arrange works for our ensemble, which comprised many tuned instruments, including the rare bass marimba. They had to find a full orchestral score, transpose the alto and tenor clef instruments and combine as much material as possible for all our players. This was all a new grounding for otherwise simple percussion players to understand the intricacies of a complex score. It sounded truly amazing, just like a symphony orchestra. We played every year in the foyer at the Barbican centre in London and had a huge audience of normal concertgoers who were proceeding to the later concerts of the LSO, LPO etc. One notable example was the performance of an outstanding student, Andrew Knox, who transcribed the last movement of the Mendelssohn violin concerto for the marimba (with a xylophone at the top for the high Es etc) and performed with astonishing virtuosity and musicality every night that could easily be compared with Oistrakh, Perlman and the like. Beethoven's Pathetique sonata, Rossini and Glinka overtures as well as Mozart symphonies were involved, as were Bach Toccatas and Fugues, Elton John and Billy Joel classics and new compositions by the boys. With my contacts still there in London, we could gain easy access to the Royal Festival Hall, Royal Albert Hall, Abbey Road studios, Henry Wood Hall etc.—all this now not possible with security as tight as ever.

A fantastic experience for them all. None of them had been out of Australia and for them each journey and occasion was an eye-opening experience. Some brought their parents, who went on to travel around Europe while we worked, and many I know still return on a regular basis.

Almost every one of the situations mentioned could never be considered in Hong Kong, certainly not the one involving the sausage, but we have all grown up since then to become pillars of society.

1A. Receiving gold medal for piano solo from Mayor of Luton.

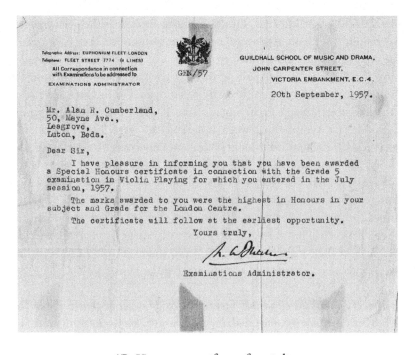

1B. Honours certificate for violin.

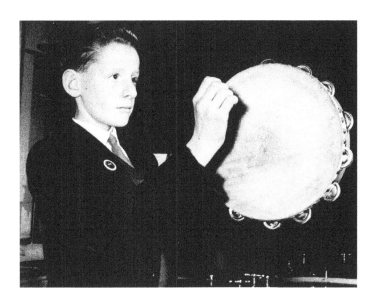

2A. Little cherub.

2B. Young Alan at the piano.

3A. Scales and Arpeggios – "a complete waste of time".

3B. Trying to look relaxed.

THE ROYAL COLLEGE OF MUSIC

INDIVIDUAL STUDIES FOR THE YEAR SEPTEMBER, 1965, TO JULY, 1966

Cumberland

Subject _____ Piano _____ Professor _____ Mr. Dawkes _____

He has made very good use of his time and broadened his knowledge of the repertoire considerably. H.D.

2. Subject _____ Percussion _____ Professor _____ Mr. H.W. Taylor _____

His ability is exceptional as a Timpanist in so short a period of study. Percussion however, covers a very wide field and he has been uneager to practise in particular, the Side-drum; an accomplishment that eludes so many. Easily the best student I have had over the years. HWTaylor.

3. Subject _____ Theory _____ Professor _____ Mr. Barlow _____

Too many missed lessons for progress.

4A. "Uneager to practise?" Never!

4B. Peter Fry, left handed, had no such difficulty with his flies.

5A. "In costume" (L-R) Alan Cumberland, Nigel Pinkett, John Foley, Malcolm Hall.

...displeasure by his expensive way of living, in Love with *Angelica*	John Stride
Scandal, his Friend, a free Speaker	Robert Lang
Tattle, a half-witted Beau, vain of his Amours, yet valuing himself for Secrecy	Laurence Olivier
Ben, *Sir Sampson's* younger Son, half Home-bred, and half Sea-bred, designed to marry *Miss Prue*	Colin Blakely
Foresight, an illiterate old Fellow, peevish and positive, superstitious, and pretending to understand Astrology, etc, Uncle to *Angelica*	Miles Malleson
Jeremy, Servant to *Valentine*	Tom Kempinski
Trapland, a Scrivener	Harry Lomax
Snap, a Bailiff	Mike Gambon
Buckram, a Lawyer	Peter Cellier
Steward to *Sir Sampson*	Reginald Green
Servant to *Foresight*	David Hargreaves
Blackamoor, Servant to *Sir Sampson*	Roy Holder
Robin, Butler to *Foresight*	Terence Knapp
Singer	Leonard Whiting
Musicians	Alan Cumberland, John Foley, Malcolm Hall, Nigel Pinkett

Love
for
Love

William Congreve

5B. " *Love for Love*"- The National Theatre 1965.

6A. AC with Elvis Presley and colleagues.

6B. "Wooden Sticks" – Glyndebourne 1985.

7A. This is just our runabout helicopter behind.

EASY DOES IT—Allen Cumberland, a member of the London Symphony, takes a preliminary lesson in water skiing from Mrs. Carleton Williams. The Ormond Beach Ski Club was host to about 30 LSO members Sunday afternoon at the Ski Club jump by the Rockefeller Memorial Bridge in Ormond Beach. There will be another indoctrination class this Sunday for LSO members.

7B. The lesson was fruitless.
7C. Lovely breasts.

ALAN OFF DUTY

WITH A RESOUNDING CLASH
... Alan Cumberland at work

8A. 24 inch arm breaking cymbals.

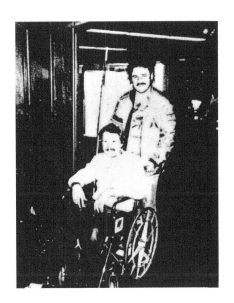

8B. Two juvenile delinquents.

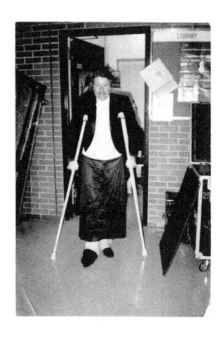

9A. Tails, hospital pyjamas and a nylon slip just before Mahler 5.

9B. Selling dish mops to the Chinese.

10A. Mstislav Rostropovich.

10B. Los Caracoles, Barcelona.

11A. Sunburnt in 43°, Perth WA.

11B. Enjoying a quiet beer at Qld Con with Gordon Hughes (L)
and Brett Carvolth (R).

12A. My percussion ensemble in Brisbane 1989.
(L-R) Tim Corkeron, David Quinn, Darren Hulcombe, Susan Vick, Alan Cumberland, Tania Savage, Phil Usher, Brett Carvolth, Jason Hawkins.
(*Absent*- David Adelt)

12B. Qld Conservatorium Percussion Ensemble 1994.
(L-R) Brett Carvolth, Jason Hawkins, Lucas Gordon,
Tanja Hafenstein, Gordon Hughes, David Quinn, Andrew Knox.

13A. LPO Concert Programmes.

13B. *"Old Mates"*
(L-R) Simon Carrington (LPO Principal Timpani),
Neil Percy (LSO Principal Percussion),
Alan Cumberland,
John Chimes (BBC SO Principal Timpani).

14. David Morbey with his timpani sticks.

Dr. h. c. Klaus Tennstedt

Roesoll 13
2305 Heikendorf
Telefon 0431/242170

June 24. 87

Dear Alan,

I ate but with love. First: you are a bad boy and
we got a shock. Now we have to listen to the old
records to hear you.
But Klaus do understand you and all our good
wishes are with you. We hope your decision was
the best for you and your family.
Klaus feel better and better and on Aug. the 15th
he will conduct the Proms-concert. Hopefull the
start for a healthy future.
Take all our best wishes — with my bad English —

sincerely

Inge + Klaus

15. Farewell to the LPO letter from Klaus and Inge Tennstedt.

Never indeed have I heard those four first movement knocks raised so securely to the status of melody, not least whenever the turn came of Alan Cumberland, a very special timpanist. As for Perlman's playing, here was that unity of heart and mind which is specific to our art and defies definition, except perhaps for the cleverness in reserving mere display for judiciously selected spots of the cadenza.

16A. Five knocks actually.

16B. "Timpani supposed to be playing here and it's too loud".

16C. What a talent (the one on the left).

17A. A drink in the bar? Perhaps not.

17B. Lion's roar.

18. London Philharmonic (Royal Festival Hall) *(Photo by Terry Hall)*.

19. Final LPO Concert, April 1987.

20A. Conducting the HKAPA Orchestra.

20B. Hong Kong Lunch (L-R) Sandy Leung, Alan Cumberland, Emily Cheng Mei Kwan, HO Ming-yan, Rainice Lai, Mandy Lo, Wai Man Raymond Vong.

21A. *"Life is for Living"* Alan Cumberland & Keith Millar.

21B. *"Pillars of Society"*
(L-R) Simon Carrington (LPO Timpanist), Alan Cumberland,
Larry Reese (NZSO Timpanist), Andy Barclay (LPO Principal
Percussionist), Keith Millar (LPO Percussionist).

Part Two

'A timpanist is a person who stands or sits at the back of the orchestra hitting two, three or four drums of different sizes according to the music on their stand'.

This, I believe is how many people including most concert-goers, teachers, organists, singers and, perish the thought, some conductors see it. In my view, timpanists can be placed in one of three categories.

(i)   Those who play rather loudly throughout to attract attention, irrespective of the nature of the work or the orchestration

There are many of these, simply having large instruments in front of them that create a feeling of power so they may dominate the proceedings. In my younger days, many principal timpanists of otherwise excellent and renowned orchestras were just like this, completely ruining the contributions of the other members and oblivious to anything other than the noise they were making. These "musical thugs" totally wreck a performance. It is quite wrong they are paid good money for this. Although the situation has changed dramatically over the past forty years or so, there are still sadly many players in this category.

(ii)   Those who play exactly what is written on their part (*p* is soft and *ff* is very loud)

Players like this are totally inadequate when it comes to being part of the orchestra. They may as well not be there. Sadly again, there are all too many players in this category too.

(iii)   Those who understand the meaning of interpretation, musicality and sensitivity

Now this is what being a great timpanist is really about. It is imperative that the player is familiar with the size of orchestra they are dealing with, the character of the music, the matter of interpretation and the techniques of how to enhance the entire performance. I see in the concert program of many orchestras under "orchestral members", "solo timpanist". For me, a timpanist is an integral part of the orchestra, not a soloist. He is there to complement the sounds of the other members and enrich the performance.

Standing or sitting?

When holding masterclasses in the different countries, I put this question to the assembled company. Invariably, I get the response from one or two that they always stand "because their teachers tell them to", some feel it gives them more freedom, most, as the timpani "soloist" wish to be seen by as many people as possible and others feel they can see the conductor and he can see them more clearly.

Some participants suggest that they sit for contemporary works or where tuning is required, otherwise they are happy to stand for classical works or those needing no additional tuning. The vast majority (every one of my students) I am pleased to say, tell me they sit at all times. Maybe *their* teachers tell them to sit, or perhaps they are just lazy? I must add here that I always played without shoes, even at concerts, as this gave me intimate contact with the pedals. Many American concert halls have no risers, so the comment above about being seen and seeing the conductor was relevant, but one must remember that it is not *always* a good idea to see who is on the box (especially if he is Hungarian).

A good set-up, as with every other instrument is paramount. Both feet on the ground (pedals for us), height of stool, placement of back-rest, hands and arms in the most natural position etc.

The stool

The timpanist's chair itself is a vital part of our set up. It makes sense that we all like to be as comfortable as possible when playing our instrument. A high rigid kitchen or bar stool is clearly not the answer as with the necessary constant sphinctoral movement could certainly induce haemorrhoids. We would agree, I feel sure, that the swivel type is a good choice. Office furniture stores have a wide variety of models, but none in my experience had anything remotely resembling the one I needed. So I set out to design my own and have used the same model for my entire playing career.

Firstly it must not have wheels! A solid base with a few supports (in my case, five) to grip the floor is good. It must be sturdy but not immovable. The lower part and height adjustable circular foot rest must be compact enough to avoid interference with the pedals. The seat, to avoid bed sores, must not contain thick layers of foam rubber, and should be large enough to allow first class comfort in long *tacet* periods and firm enough for perching on the front in the playing position. It should have a tilt facility, forward and back. Again, pay attention to the type of covering—it must obviously be made of non-slip material. Arm rests, although welcome in the sleeping position for Bruckner symphonies and for reading the newspaper during rehearsals, are not suitable for every other reason. The back rest must be completely manoeverable with a firm but again adaptable support for the small of your back. This is only my preference, as what is good for me is not necessarily good for everyone else, so you should choose the stool which best suits your needs.

Sitting with the feet on the pedals gives us the maximum re-tuning time, the ability to execute glissandi and above all, the opportunity to constantly alter the pitch, however small that adjustment might be. The pedals are after all, simply extensions of your feet. Feel and look comfortable, look, listen and be totally confident with every movement from your driving position at the back of the orchestra.

Concept of sound

Playing the timpani is not simply the matter of hitting a drum. The player should have a definite concept of the sound of every note he wishes to produce. This varies greatly from person to person.

Where to strike the drum? Finding the "sweet spot" is crucial, allowing you to produce the purest tone you can. If the head is set up perfectly, an identical sound should be produced with both sticks equidistant from that central spot creating an almost parallel position of the arms. Contrary to the belief of a number of my colleagues, it is completely unnecessary to strike the drum with both sticks at the same place. Great care must always be taken with the playing area, especially as the drums get smaller where the striking position is critical. It is usually necessary to actually look where you are hitting the drum, particularly with the "piccolo" as the right (in my case) hand is "out of position".

Then there is the sound that conductors say they want to hear. It impresses the orchestra you know, when they say something "technical" about the timpani. Without mentioning names, I am sure most haven't a clue. They have read it somewhere. (It's the same when they ask for harder sticks. "No problem", we say, pretend to substitute them, and then use precisely the same ones. "Bravo, that's a better sound"). It is really up to the player who would consider the size and repertoire of his orchestra, the ideal drum to play and the sticks with which to do it. I have no intention of mentioning baroque instruments in this book, simply because I know nothing about them. The only comment I might make is that I did not like playing or hearing modern timpani being played with wooden sticks alongside conventional trumpets and other winds. One style or the other for me, not a mixture. An occasion did occur some years ago when I had to play a number of performances of Mozart's *Idomeneo* for the Glyndebourne production followed by a BBC Prom. Simon Rattle asked me if I minded using wooden sticks. Naturally I said I *would* mind, but as Simon and I are good mates, the deal was that he provided me with some Famous Grouse whisky, which he did.

I spent most of my professional life in London with the LPO, whose "home" was the Royal Festival Hall. Now this was the most awful place with an acoustic akin to a space capsule. Mercifully, this has now changed. The LPO has a reputation for playing the standard repertoire we all know and love with a full rich tone. Amongst our staple diet of Elgar, Bruckner, Mahler, Strauss, etc., performances without this are deeply unsatisfying. But the London orchestras all seemed at the time to have the facility and experience to produce the sonority required in such an unforgiving place. As the new kid on the block, it was beyond my comprehension that a full, projecting sound of great quality was not produced simply by playing louder. There is a lot more to it than that. The sound and tone must be drawn from the drum, not hammered into it.

On our many overseas tours, the LPO performed in some of the very best (and many of the very worst) concert halls in the world. The ones at the top of my list were the Musikverein in Vienna, the Philharmonie in Berlin, the Carnegie in New York and the Concertgebouw in Amsterdam. Sadly there was no British hall that ever came close to the fine acoustics in the other countries. It was always interesting to note though, that when hearing the NYPO or VPO, BPO, CSO or the Concertgebouw at the Royal Festival Hall, they seemed to almost have to force their instruments to fill the auditorium with their beautiful sound. On the other hand we had to do just the opposite in their lovely halls to keep our tone quality and sheer volume under control. I was always after the highest quality sound and tried every manner of things, all of which are covered in this book, to produce it.

Choice of instruments

There are far more instrument makers now than forty years ago, but we still had a choice. Starting my career on Premiers (because I didn't know any better) I soon changed over to Ludwigs, as they could allow me to produce the rich fuller sound I wanted. The pedals were so much easier to manage and the gauges unobtrusive and perfectly placed (not any more). I discussed this at length with Kurt-Hans Goedicke, the principal timpanist in the LSO who was most helpful to me at the time. We both agreed that Ludwigs were the best option, but then what about sizes? Whatever the manufacturer, the large percentage of orchestras and timpanists around the world would have, and still do, the equivalent of 32", 29", 26" and 23". We both chose 2 x 32",

29", 26" and a 23" for the very high stuff. Kurt and I had slightly different ranges on our identically sized timpani. Mine were approximately

32", C – A   32", F – Db   29", B – E   26", E – A   23", F – C

As you see, the heads were tuned to the highest end of their ranges, providing a purer sound and avoiding any "flapping". They were always tuned to slightly above the extremes of their range for obvious reasons. I would never extend that range, not even by a semitone as I and the instruments would not be comfortable. It is odd that both the 32s were happy within their designated ranges. For A and E, I would use the second rather than the lower 32 with the 29. With this set up, there were two works I could not manage with the standard four drums: Strauss *Burlesque* (A D E F) and Shostakovich's Symphony No. 10, #4 (B C D Eb), so another drum was introduced. For Beethoven's Symphony No. 8, I would remove the 29 to leave me with the two 32s and the 26, the second 32 providing the low F for #4 as it did in the ninth symphony for #2.

On one occasion, I received a communication from another established manufacturer, which had just launched a new model of timpani. The founder and managing director asked me to assess their instruments, and flew me to his factory where I was entertained to a fine lunch. In the afternoon, I was given a thorough tour and a chance to play these gleaming models. They were most impressive and the heads had been tuned perfectly. The notes produced were true, the pedals were almost identical to the Ludwig type and the instruments seemed ideal. I was suitably impressed and more than happy to agree to give them a trial with the LPO. A new set of instruments was shipped to the UK and I agreed to assess them over a period of a few months. The orchestral attendants, responsible for moving the drums to each venue (which was often three different places in one day) were unimpressed to say the least, as they were rather heavier than the Ludwigs. Much heavier in fact! Representatives from the company paid regular visits to our rehearsals and concerts at the Royal Festival Hall, which was the major concert hall and "shop window" for us all. The instruments were easy to play and sounded very good indeed. I asked my colleagues to have a listen in various parts of the auditorium to assess the qualities and tone produced. I also went out myself whilst one of them stood in for me. We all shared the same feeling. We simply could not hear them. There was no projection whatsoever. We all tried different sticks every time to no avail. The company thought we were being over critical and suggested the sound was perfectly good. They offered me a complimentary set of five drums if I was to use them in the orchestra, a kind gesture which I unfortunately had to turn down. These drums are perfectly good for teaching, for use in recording studios and smaller concert halls. I have never had any hesitation in recommending these instruments to the various institutions in which I have taught.

One more thing which is definitely worth mentioning—placement of the music stand. This may seem trivial, but it certainly is not. I have noticed many players with their stand between two drums directly over the top of the heads. Although easier to see and more convenient for page turning, this effectively acts as a damper and interferes with the tone quality. When orchestral risers are used, a good position for the stand is behind the drums, just below the rims, allowing you to just see the bottom line of the score. This enables the sound to project, the audience to see what is going on and a good view of the conductor (if so desired).

Choice of heads

Years ago, the player could simply choose between calf and plastic heads, quite different with each manufacturer, but now with the introduction of changing formulae from many new companies, a far wider range of products is available. Yes, the choice of heads was limited, but I found the Remo plastic/nylon type were the most reliable and suitable for the sound I wished to produce. There were no Renaissance or other decent heads around at that time that I liked.

As the Remo heads were manufactured overseas, I had to be sure that every head was perfectly "true", so I was pleased to have a reliable source, Lloyd McCausland at the factory. Even with the perfect head, it had to be fitted correctly. This was done then with our ears and not with the tuning devices currently available. With the extreme conditions to which the drums were exposed, on the tarmac at O'Hare airport in the middle of winter, in the blazing 43 degree heat of Perth, Western Australia, the 100% humidity at Hong Kong and so on, it was a credit to both Remo and Ludwig that the heads and the drums (with only padded nylon covers to protect them) were so durable. I suppose we should be prepared for any eventuality.

One for which I definitely wasn't, however, was the celebration of Australian entrepreneur Christopher Skases' fortieth birthday party, a lavish occasion attended by film stars, tycoons, politicians and the like, held at the new Sheraton Mirage hotel at the Gold Coast in Queensland. Professors and students from the Conservatorium were engaged to play at this huge event. We were to perform Handel's *Music for the Royal Fireworks* to the promenading guests, accompanied of course by real fireworks. Several jumbo barrels of gunpowder were attached underneath the eaves of the roof where the orchestra was set and were to discharge powerful jets of fireworks away from us across the sea. This was demonstrated with a mini trial run at the rehearsal. It would be quite spectacular later with all the barrels operating. One tiny detail that the organizers had unfortunately failed to take into account was that as the tide turns, the sea breeze intensifies and blows in the opposite direction—towards us! No sooner had we begun, the problems started. The noise and the smoke from the fireworks were unbearable, so nobody could see or hear us anyway, but even worse, flames were beginning to spread alarmingly across the stage. We were catching fire. My colleague's hair was burning, the clarinetist's music was aflame and I noticed brown smoldering plastic on my (hired) timpani heads. But we continued to play. The show must go on. Very soon though, somebody shouted "All off!" and we were gone. It was around eighteen months later that we received compensation for our ruined white tuxedos. The timpani heads were replaced.

Pedals

Pedal action is so very important for complete comfort and accuracy with tuning. Although I managed with the Premier type for some years, I was never entirely happy with the sharp angle of the ankle needed to release the pedal and the sheer strength required on the smaller drums. Even worse is the side kick release of many models which present unnecessary difficulties to allow accurate playing of demanding or chromatic passages and more importantly to constantly adjust the pitch of each note. The fine tuner with the handle at the side of the drum is useless when playing a roll and however skilful he may be with his feet, the sideways/up and down action throws the player off balance when engaged in this act. Unfortunately for me, as every note is subject to the tiniest change I would look and feel very awkward remaining in this unnatural position for the whole piece. The "accelerator" type Ludwig action presented no such problems—it was comfortable for the foot to stay there as long as required, the minutest change of pitch was possible and the overall playing position was not affected. The heel is not the most sensitive part of the body, but it plays an integral part in shifting the pitch downward. Some attention to this should be paid by less experienced players. Practising a few chromatic scales up and down on the four drums would be useful. As we know, tones and semitones are not the same distance apart on every drum, and particular care must be taken with the smaller instruments. Accuracy is of paramount importance when playing pedal passages in p and pp as the hands will be played delicately and the ankles played firmly, as per normal. Familiarity with every interval on each drum is essential.

Gauges

Gauges are essential for all timpanists, even those with vast experience and knowledge of every millimeter of the path of the pedal. The *Intermezzo* from Bartok's *Concerto for Orchestra* springs to mind, where changes both up and down are required. The unobtrusive positioning of the compact gauges of the Ludwigs was good with the two middle drums having them in an adjacent position, clearly visible to the player. Care had to be taken that the gold letters were "bent" sufficiently to prevent them moving. Sadly, I find the gauges on their modern instruments far too clumsy and obtrusive. When setting the gauge before a performance, it is advisable to have some leeway at the extremes of the range allowing for pitch changes with the atmosphere in the halls. The gauges were accurate when ascending but not so when coming down, so it is imperative that the pedal be brought to the heel-down position before depressing to the required pitch, however quick that change may be.

Choice of sticks

The commercial sticks available to us all those years ago were quite simply useless. Most of the older players were using sticks they made themselves for calf heads and were totally ineffective on plastic. There were the aforementioned "dish mops", those with a seam which was "audible", those hard felt ones that created an extraneous noise when the head was struck especially in *p*, those with uneven canes and ones which were more like tree trunks, allowing little control and "touch" from the player. The German sticks in theory were good, but with an excess of felt around the core tended to be just too fluffy which dulled the tone somewhat. With the very light bamboo, the player had to work harder than I felt necessary. I was flattered to receive many offers from people, wishing to create the perfect stick for me and tried many different types with various shafts, cores and coverings, some of which were useful for some effects, but none with which I was totally satisfied.

It was with considerable relief then, that a private student of mine brought along a few pairs of sticks he had "created" for me. These were made specifically for my size and shape of hand, grip and playing technique. The weight, balance and durability were all important for me with my heavy working schedule and no expense was spared in the preparation of this vital part of the timpanists' equipment. The prototype sticks were all made of a dowel shaft with a rather rough felt covering the cork, felt or wooden core.

The most important feature was, like the German sticks, they had no seam or obvious place where the felt was attached. Unfortunately, the sticks tended to break or splinter too often and so were quickly replaced by a bamboo shaft. This was polished and looked impressive, but it was all too easy to lose the grip when rolling, allowing the stick to fly away. Again, this was addressed and a not-so-slippery lacquer applied. Then there was the centre and the covering. Many different types of core were tried and wood was chosen for everyday playing whilst other materials were used for special effects. The covering was all important as there should be no audible sound when the head is struck. With no seams to concern me, the stick could be held in any position around the shaft, so any wear in one particular place was of no consideration. The material used to cover the head of the sticks was a fine felt-like yarn which was woven around the core in a "spinning machine", the method of which remains a top secret. Many pairs of these sticks were tried with the manufacturer sitting in at rehearsals and concerts. Although I had a choice of a wide range of sticks, I only used a standard set of five or so pairs on a regular basis, and most often, only two pairs. Even playing around eighteen sessions in an average week, often with heavy repertoire, the sticks were unbreakable and the felt surprisingly long lasting. My student's name was David Morbey, now one of the world's finest manufacturers of timpani sticks.

Grip of sticks

This affects the style of playing as well as the action involved. There are basically two types of grip: thumbs up or palms down. The thumbs-up method is used widely in some countries but the UK most usually adopts the fingers-up position. The thumbs-up position involves fingers in addition to the wrists but for me the wrists-down action is more flexible. I suggest to my students that they might try to adopt as similar a position as possible for all the instruments in our department. I would liken the actual grip of holding a pencil or a baton in the place that the balance is good and that the stick will respond precisely to your movements. Although this was by far the normal position, it didn't mean I never turned my hands over. For many single notes, including the opening of Beethoven's violin concerto (with one hand), the last note of his symphony 3 #2, and the last C# of Bartok's *Concerto for Orchestra* #1, it felt better. I don't know why.

As with many instruments, discomfort is part of the job. Violinists and violists have that familiar red mark on their necks where the chin or shoulder rest digs in, cellists sore inner thighs, brass players have a red "passionate kissing" ring around their lips, marimba players calluses in between their fingers and we have blisters or painful areas on the fingers where the sticks have been rubbing (in addition to the red passionate kissing ring around their lips). Now I hear you all saying there must be something drastically wrong with my grip. Maybe, but try a three-week tour, concerts every night, alternating overture Tannhauser/Bruckner 4, and overture Tannhauser/Sibelius 2. It was no use, my index fingers used to bleed, and when damping the blood would drip onto the heads and if I was not careful onto my white shirt and cummerbund. I tried everything from band-aids and gloves to "invisible skin" and specially prescribed ointment. The only remedy I could see was to have a co-principal!

Gloves were essential when glass was involved in an unfortunate accident. A few days before the smash, I had taken delivery of a Fiat 125S, a deceptively brisk vehicle. At rehearsal earlier in the week, Vernon Handley, the conductor, suggested I put sand bags in the boot to help with stability, as the relationship between the lightweight body and the powerful engine was asking for trouble from some "hoon" like me. I foolishly ignored his advice. On my way home after dinner with Peter Chrippes some days later, I approached the local chicane at a speed which was not appropriate for the drizzle-coated road surface and spun the car a few times hitting other stationary vehicles in its path. Seat belts were not compulsory in those days, and I went clean through the windscreen and slid on my front along the road. Mercifully there was no traffic coming from the opposite direction. This was a mess. I clambered up and felt bumps on my head and had painful hands which were grazed, cut and bleeding from the shards of glass. My car was a total write-off and three other residents' parked vehicles badly damaged. The police arrived, took details and drove me home, leaving the remains of the Fiat to be transported to the wrecker's yard. Despite a sleepless night, I was determined not to let a silly accident like this get in the way and turned up as usual, albeit stiffly this time, for a painful rehearsal of Vaughan Williams' fourth symphony with Sir Adrian at RFH (I learned my lesson the hard way that speed was not everything and so after a few days with a hired car, bought a Jaguar 3.8MK2).

Sticking

There is much debate between students and teachers here. How many times did keen students sitting behind me in concerts all over the place ask me why I used a particular sticking in a particular passage? I had no idea why I used it except that it was perfectly natural for me. Unless a passage was unusually complicated, I never needed to work out and write the sticking in the part. Just a L here and a R there was enough. I have seen so many parts with

LLRLRL LRRLLRL etc. Together with totally unnecessary tuning directions, the actual notes became obliterated. All that is needed for retuning is a small arrow or line from the existing note to the name of the new note. Try to leave the part as clean as possible.

I return to the subject of "pleasing to watch". I find that if a player uses the "wrong" stick to get to another drum, even in simple passages, it seems as though he is sight-reading or struggling in some way. A paradiddle is usually the answer.

I was never in favour of cross sticking—moving quickly from side to side was quite successful rather than crossing over. Beethoven was good training with his Symphony No. 1 (Figure 1), #3 and Symphony No. 8, #4 (Figure 2). My main reason was that when the stick is crossed, it takes fractionally more time to reach its destination, thus marginally affecting the rhythm.

Figure 1. Bar 44-127, Beethoven Symphony No. 1, third movement.

Figure 2. End of Beethoven Symphony No. 8, fourth movement.

There were exceptions naturally where 'knitting' is required, one being the end of Berlioz's *Symphonie Fantastique* (Figure 3).

Figure 3. End of Berlioz's *Symphonie Fantastique*.

An excerpt from the same work frequently set for auditions, and one that so called "learned" panel members, in addition to conductors, are keen to express their wide knowledge of the timpani is the "March to the Scaffold" (Figure 4). If an appropriate speed is chosen, it is perfectly possible to play all the sextuplets with the RH and the main beats with the left, or even R&LRLRLR R&LRLRLR R&L etc, but as the dynamic increases and the conductor and nearby audience have lost interest, then forget about the double strokes on the main beats and just play RLRLRL RLRLRL R etc. *Read this all in reverse if you are a 'leftie'.*

IV.

Gang zum Hochgericht.
Marche au Supplice.   The Procession to the Stake.

Figure 4. 'March to the Scaffold' from Berlioz's *Symphonie Fantastique*.

Beethoven Symphony No. 9 #2 is best executed with RRL, RRL etc to achieve the perfect dotted rhythm and "feel" (Figure 5).

Figure 5. E – H, Beethoven Symphony No. 9, second movement.

82

On a slightly different note regarding sticking, I was to play Bartok's *Music for Strings, Percussion and Celeste* (Figure 6).

Figure 6. Bar 26- 44, Bartok's *Music for Strings, Percussion and Celeste.*

Having played the famous passage at fig 26 in #4 many times, each time without a hint of a problem, a bald Hungarian conductor happened to be on the box on this occasion. Now he should have known this piece better than most, but, as he and I didn't share a particularly close relationship he obviously chose to take this at a ridiculously fast speed rendering the passage unplayable (by me anyway). It was just a mess. So, on the way for lunch wondering what to do, I played the part with my hands on imaginary timpani, actually the dashboard of my car, whilst waiting at traffic lights. No worries! I soon twigged that my fingers were then close to the "drum" and when using sticks, they were far away. So I turned around, went back to the Festival Hall and tried it out. I could play seemingly without difficulty at a tempo even Solti wouldn't dare to take. So there was only one answer and that was to hold the sticks halfway down the shaft. This was still not good enough so I tried with my fingers almost touching the felt. Magic. It worked every time. So come the evening I used that method. It looked ghastly and sounded absolutely shocking. Hard work and embarrassing, but it somehow worked. The conductor didn't notice a thing. That *was* a surprise.

Quick changes of stick, usually involving felt and wood, as in Strauss' *Don Juan* are made that much easier if the normal sticks are almost thrown into the stick case at the side and the wooden ones taken from between the legs. To avoid injuries to sensitive parts, do ensure there are no splinters on the shafts before using this technique. Playing with the reverse ends of the sticks is not to be recommended as any tone quality is completely lost.

Figure 7. Beginning of Strauss' *Don Juan*.

Rhythm

The timpanist must have an excellent sense rhythm and pulse. Many unfortunately do not possess this prerequisite for the job. You will notice that I wrote "excellent" rather than "perfect" rhythm. It may surprise you to know that rhythm can be bent a little at times. Let me give you an example. In Beethoven's Symphony No. 1 #2 (Figure 8), the dotted rhythm can be exaggerated to show a clear difference between that and the accompanying triplets in the first violins. Similarly, in his Symphony No. 7 #1, and other dotted duple time passages of which he was so fond, the relentless rhythm is especially difficult to maintain, not so much for us, but for the winds and strings. I found that if I "clipped" the semiquavers each time, it helped the music to bounce along and at the same time, without most of the others realising it, encouraged them to similarly elongate the dotted quaver, thus fractionally shortening the semiquaver.

Figure 8. End of Beethoven Symphony No. 1, second movement.

Similarly effective "stretching" of longer notes can be employed in Brahms, R. Strauss, Elgar, Wagner, etc., where quavers must be given their full length. A good example of this is in Brahms

Symphony No. 1 #4 after E and around G (Figure 9) where the quavers can be noticeably long to contrast with the simultaneous triplets in other parts of the orchestra.

Figure 9. D-F, Brahms Symphony No. 1, fourth movement.

On Strauss operas again, there is a most peculiar passage in *Die Schweigsame Frau* which is definitely worth a look. Act I, after fig. 31 (Figure 10). At first glance it appears quite innocuous, but then that little 3/4 time signature right underneath the 2/4, cunningly disguised with tiny print could cause the heart to miss a beat at the first rehearsal. The second trumpet and timps are in 2/4 whilst the rest of the orchestra (and conductor) are in 3/4.

Figure 10. Act I, fig. 29-34, Strauss' *Die Schweigsame Frau*.

Rhythm is equally important in rests. I always did (and still do) feel the rests in the throat with an "eh", with a click of the tongue, or with the toes. Anything that keeps a firm sense of pulse. This is a rather annoying habit when listening to recorded music.

Pitch

Let's take a look at a couple of examples where a slight adjustment of the pitch really makes a difference. The two middle drums are set to Eb and Bb for the overture to Mozart's *The Magic Flute*, but the second Eb is not the same pitch as the opening one. As wind players in particular will tell us, every note should be moved slightly to fit with the rest of the chord. Just because we play the timpani, it doesn't mean the rule does not apply to us. Minor 3rds must go up and major 3rds come down, perfect 5ths up and minor 7ths down. In most instances, even the keenest ear will be unable to detect these tiny changes (beware of Boulez), but for the Mozart, then the second Eb must go up for the C minor chord, returning to normal for the third chord. Take Mahler's first symphony #3—the D's and A's change throughout as the different instruments, each with their own characteristics are introduced, just like the B's and F#'s and high F's and C's in the *ben sostenuto* sections of Tchaikovsky No. 4 #1. Pay particular attention to this in Beethoven, where we are not always at the bottom of the chord. Know where you are in every chord. Use your feet as string players use their fingers and wind players their lips and slides. This rule applies throughout all repertoire. (I found that the opening Db roll in Dvorak Symphony No. 9 #2 and the Eb roll in the solo of Shostakovich Symphony No.1 moved all over the place). So, FEET ON THE PEDALS AT ALL TIMES.

Demanding chromatic parts
These excerpts are no longer as scary as they must have been a hundred years ago, in the case of Strauss' *Der Rosenkavalier* with the advent of pedals that can cope with the quick changes. "Rosenkav" is perhaps the most frequently asked excerpt at timpani auditions and is quite straightforward.

I was a little naughty here in filling in all the empty bars with the appropriate notes (Figure 11).

It gave me something extra to do and of course nobody (except the percs) knew.

Figure 11. Edited timpani part of Strauss' *Der Rosenkavalier*.

The *Intermezzo interrotto* from the *Concerto for Orchestra* by Bartok is another old favourite. Each player has his own way of pedaling this but mine was like Figure 12.

Figure 12. Bartok's *Intermezzo interrotto from Concerto for Orchestra*.

Janàček's *Aus Einem Totenhaus* is a little more challenging (Figure 13).

The passage 5 before fig. 7 is possible with minimum changes if the starting notes are F Db Eb Ab (A). Feet on Eb and Ab. The third bar just needs the Ab to go down to Gb, then the Eb up to E. Then one before 7, Db down to C and then to B. Simple. The F# (Gb) is already there. B down to Bb and F# down to F in the two bars rest. Feet on top two. E to F and A to Bb. After that low F and Bb, all you need is A and Eb, with the A going to Bb. One empty bar to find C# and high F#. C# down to B. DONE!

In this whole passage, everything is syncopated except the Db on the first beat three bars before 7. With an accent on this note, it helps everybody. Learn the part and count religiously.

Figure 13. Fig. 6 – fig. 9, Janàček's *Aus Einem Totenhaus*.

Back to Strauss' opera *Die Schweigsame Frau* (Figure 14). which is another naughty little one right from the "Potpourri" at the beginning. Although the changes on the first page are quite quick, they *are* possible (remember the golden rule—pedal on as few drums as possible.) Two bars before M is another matter. It would be simpler if another low drum was introduced, but as the music is *allegro molto* and rather noisy at that point, I saw no reason to do that. It does, however, require a little cheating. There is plenty of time in the seven bars rest to tune to Ab A D F#, feet on top two. Quickly down to Db and F in bar 2, then again quickly down to C and E in bar 3. If you can

89

manage to get the Ab down to a G at the same time, then well and good, but at that tempo it is not realistically possible, so instead of the first G, hit the Ab and then make sure you tune down to a G for the final note. In this way, only one note is out of tune, but with everything else that is going on, no-one will know any difference.

Figure 14. Letter D-N Strauss' *Die Schweigsame Frau*.

Fig. 118 (Figure 15) in Act 1 is *definitely* worth a look beforehand. There are of course many ways of coping with these passages depending on drum sizes and pedal action, not to mention the foot and stick technique of the player.

Figure 15. Fig. 116 – fig. 120, Strauss' *Die Schweigsame Frau*. Act II.

Drums in the 'wrong' order

I have seen some players use a set up of B, C, Eb, D for the end of Shostakovich Symphony No. 10. It may be easier to play with the drums in this order, but for me loses the visual effect of chromaticism leaving the audience wondering whether this indeed was the of D Eb C B theme of the work.

In the fourth scene of Strauss' *Salome* (Figure 16), a different order of drums is absolutely necessary to allow the player to cope with the scalic passages at speed. Bar 298 could be Ab C Bb D, and one way of getting around bar 362 would be to use C D Db Eb. This arrangement would not be possible with my personal set up, so other drums must be used. Failing that, and bearing in mind we are usually out of sight in the pit for this, maybe C D Eb would do, with some nifty footwork for the D and Db?

91

Figure 16. Bar 298-302 and Bar 362-369, Strauss' *Salome*.

Damping

Damping can be a complete distraction for the audience.

There is absolutely no need to damp every time you see rests — many amateur players are guilty of this—it looks ridiculous, sounds stifled and interferes with the music. If you notice your sound is "leaking" into rests when everybody else has stopped, then damp. Even if you are not playing, you may need to damp your drums so they do not resonate with the brass instruments. It tends to upset them.

If quick damping is required, try it with alternate hands where possible so as not to look lop-sided. Where to damp? This is normally done with the hands or fingers in the striking position at the edge of the drum. On occasions after loud playing, it is necessary to stop the sound with both hands. In quieter passages, then a ripple-like action with the fingers and palm avoids an audible buzz. There are many instances where other methods are necessary. The effect is generally achieved with movable felt pads in the centre, not near the rim, as I see so many times. If the sound is stopped in this way, the pitch and quality of note is indeterminable. I do understand that sometimes, for example in Schubert Symphony No. 9 #3 (Figure 17), dampers need to be almost tossed away (and retrieved each time) after the articulated quavers but with deft movements by the hands, it is possible to achieve the desired effect. Quite heavy dampers are necessary here. My thighs were the most obvious place from which to work.

Figure 17. Fig. D, Schubert Symphony No. 9, third movement.

I used squarish pads taken from the (used) baize of a snooker table. Any number of these could be used for different degrees of damping in the centre with movement towards the player for more solid work. Thicker felt pads or even folded dusters would achieve a similar result.

Let's look at some specific examples which the "special" timpanist might employ.

Holst: The Planets.
Mercury needs heavy damping for the rhythm to be clear

Mahler: Symphony No. 1, #3
Although the score stipulates *gedämpft*, many players do not observe this marking. Although I wanted a smothering of the sound, a damper on both drums was not precisely what I needed. I think we would all use two different sized drums for the D and A, in my case 32" and 29". The A on the larger drum is bound to be much boomier than the D, so to achieve a similar degree of muffled sound, the weight of the dampers must be considered. I found that two layers on the D and four on the A, both in the centre, were just about right.

Sibelius: Violin concerto
Here is a composer who, like Benjamin Britten, knew exactly what he wanted with his writing for timpani—precisely placed dynamics, where to start and stop rolls, accents etc., etc. One would think that the single F six bars before 4a #1 would be a single crotchet, but he wanted a roll (Figure 18a). The single quavers eleven bars before 5 need a heavy damper. The rolls at 25 and 21 before fig 6 are separate, so a tiny accent on each one helps clarify that.

Again, clarity is of the essence five bars after fig. 11 (Figure 18b), so I employed a different technique. Try this— use a reasonably heavy damper in the middle of the drum on the D's and use a crushed roll (almost throw the sticks at the head) and shortening each one by a fraction of a second before every quaver. It is most effective. The damper should hold for the five-bar roll as the accompaniment is not loud. Heavyish dampers again for the six quaver D's that follow. I found a useful technique for the last fifteen bars was RR damp (L), RLRR damp (L) etc. This is also visually interesting and the nearest I'll ever get to looking like a kit drummer.

Figure 18a. Fig 4, 4a and 5, Sibelius' Violin concerto, first movement.

Figure 18b. Fig 11, Sibelius' Violin concerto, first movement.

94

The third movement is brilliantly written with the pulsating rhythmical duet between timps and cellos. Dampers yes, to emulate the sound of the cellos' marcato quaver and two semiquavers. I always watched the principal cellist at this point and started quite strongly to "get the thing going". I once again used the crushed, dampened technique five bars after fig. 2 and accentuated the first beat of every bar to give that extra kick (Figure 19a). Watch out for that funny looking rhythm four bars before fig. 10 (Figure 19b). There is some debate whether he wanted a roll, as printed, for the final two notes. Once again, a squashed roll does the trick.

Figure 19a. Five bars after fig. 2 – fig.3, Sibelius' Violin concerto, third movement.

Figure 19b. Fig. 9, Sibelius' Violin concerto, third movement.

Beethoven: Symphony No. 9 #4

Here's something that will complement the trumpets' staccato crotchets after fig. 7 (Figure 20). Play everything with right hand and damp only the staccato notes with the left. Give the longer ones a "little extra" just to make your point.

Figure 20. Letter F, Beethoven Symphony No. 9, fourth movement.

Bartok: Music for Strings, Percussion & Celeste

We have already discussed the embarrassing side to the Db Ab section, but let's look at clarity. Unless really heavy dampers are used, they will move and even fall away. If you have a reasonably good note on drums 1 and 4, then the first two notes could be on these outer drums with heavy damping on the middle two. Maybe in years to come, someone will invent automatic dampers?

Berlioz: Symphonie Fantastique #4

We have looked at some ideas of sticking here, but heavy damping is needed for total clarity by both timpanists. As the dynamic increases, remove them and toss to one side. It is pointless using dampers for any dynamic exceeding *f*.

Tchaikovsky: Symphony No. 4 #1

ben sostenuto—even though notes are short with rests, let them ring for full resonance and again have a damper handy for low F# so as to equalize that with the B. Whip the damper off when the dynamics grow. The B, and the C and high F in the earlier corresponding passage should not need damping if the C is on 32 and F on 26.

Musicality/interpretation

Musicality is something with which you are born or soon develop. Interpretation is entirely a personal matter. Even now, when I look back on my playing career, there are still things I would do differently today. As they say, you can't beat experience. To work in London with an everlasting stream of some of the finest musicians in the world is indeed a privilege.

Just because we have only two, three or four notes to play, it doesn't mean that we can't play them musically. We have already discussed the choice of sticks, where to strike the drum and so on and assume we are producing the best possible sound from the instrument. I suppose we should go right back to basics and look at the time signature, the style of music, the orchestration, dynamics and the like.

This book is not a manual so I have no intention, like some teachers, authors and "clinicians" of analysing every note of every piece and saying which sticks and sticking you must use. You are the timpanist, not me. Every one of us is an individual, so it is not really in anybody's best interest to look just like someone else. Every note is important, however irrelevant it might seem. Be aware of what's going on around you. Look, listen and breathe.

Here are just a few suggestions to let you know where I am coming from.
Not one of these was even noticed, let alone appreciated by Solti.

Time signature and phrasing

Let's look at the most straightforward music on paper, the classical composers. Just two or three notes to play. The first beat of the bar is almost always the most important and should be slightly stressed. As Sir Adrian Boult used to say, "avoid any bumps in the middle of the bar". In minuets, trios, in waltzes and most dances, the first beat can be more heavily marked. Always remember the first beat rule, but never let it become relentless and boring.

Beethoven: Symphony No. 1

#2 clipped rhythm as discussed and after the repeat sign do not play, but damp instead of playing the first **p** dotted semiquaver 10 and 8 before letter C (Figure 21).

Figure 21. Beginning of Beethoven Symphony No. 1, second movement.

Symphony No. 3

#1 always look out for something to make the part more interesting and bring out the semiquavers nine bars after letter Q (Figure 22).

Figure 22. Letter O-Q, Beethoven Symphony No. 3, first movement.

#2 always accent on the first beat after triplet demisemis before H (Figure 23).

Figure 23. Letter G-H, Beethoven Symphony No. 3, second movement.

#3 emphasis comes every four bars, but then in the twelfth bar, make a feature of the three crotchets. At the coda, I always phrased it in four bar sections. (Figure 24)

Figure 24. Letter A-B, Beethoven Symphony No. 3, third movement.

#4 the demisemiquaver triplets at the end are simply as fast as possible (Figure 25).

Figure 25. End of Beethoven Symphony No. 3, fourth movement.

Symphony No. 4
#2 the rhythm should be absolutely strict.

#3 again every two bars to fit the shape of the melody (Figure 26).

Figure 26. Beginning of Beethoven Symphony No. 4, third movement.

Symphony No. 5
#1 Take care not to be late every time after the quaver rests. At letter E, emphasise the last three quavers and the next crotchet to go with the trumpets (and tradition) (Figure 27).

Figure 27. Letter E, Beethoven Symphony No. 5, first movement.

#2 four bars after D and in corresponding places, emphasize first beat and in eight and nine after D the second beat (Figure 28).

Figure 28. Letter D, Beethoven Symphony No. 5, second movement.

#3 In the damped solo, a little something extra every four bars, then phrase the following bars with the firsts just to give them a little help (Figure 29).

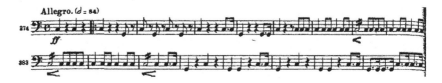

Figure 29. Letter C, Beethoven Symphony No. 5, third movement.

#4, I found that a noticeable crescendo on the semiquavers at bar 381 and an accent on the first of the quavers added a dramatic effect and was appreciated by conductors (Figure 30).

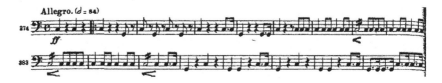

Figure 30. Bar 374-390, Beethoven Symphony No. 5, fourth movement.

Symphony No. 6
Exaggerate the dynamics for the storm. Really quite powerful.

Symphony No.7
#1 So many things in this symphony. Four bars before letter A, "wrong" notes, so mark dynamic down. Clip all the rhythms as discussed. Thirteen and eleven before letter C sounds good with a crescendo. Six before the double bar is effective with a crescendo. Three and seven after H is good to use *fp* to get out of the way of other things. At the semiquaver solo passage at the end, have two A's, one damped and the other open and switch from one to the other as it gets louder (Figure 31).

Figure 31. Bar 313-335, Beethoven Symphony No. 7, first movement.

#2 last two notes, change to C?
#3 delete the *p* note and damp instead. All first beats with accents in this

movement. Traditionally the long A roll in the trio is done with a *ffp* then a
crescendo around the sixth bar both times (Figure 32).

Figure 32. Beethoven Symphony No. 7, third movement.

#4 is full of notes, many of which are not important. Keep out of the way
when you can—it is not a timpani/trumpet concerto. At letter D, the piece
modulates into C major, so mark all these notes right down. Do observe the
specific *ff* and *sf* accents after letter H and then a good crescendo two bars
before the GP bar is effective. Between I and K these notes mean little, so
mark them almost *p*.

Symphony No. 8

As discussed before, remove drum no. 3 and have 32, 32, 26 so that no. 2 32 will accommodate both the C and F. Then the F octaves are adjacent.

#1 In the beginning feel the melody like Figure 33.

Figure 33. Beginning of Beethoven Symphony No. 8, first movement.

Whilst at this place, to clarify the rhythm on the F rolls, I just accented the beginning of each one.

The fourth bar of letter I is almost a crescendo and from the eighth bar onwards, a definite stress on all first beats is good until the last four bars (Figure 34.)

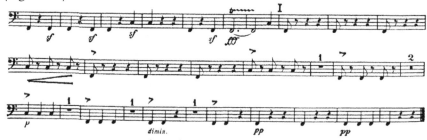

Figure 34. Beginning of Beethoven Symphony No. 8, first movement.

#4 Use the "better" no. 1 drum for everything except the crossing passages.

Symphony No. 9

#1 Whether Beethoven intended it or not, I found that to stop the first roll on the second beat and give it an accent helps punctuate the rhythm (Figure 35). This also applies to nine bars before the end. Add the effective traditional crescendo four after K. Prepare to slow a little to accommodate the other players. Make a marked difference between the quavers and demisemiquavers at the last *a tempo*. I used a paradiddle rather than crossing four bars before S.

Figure 35. Beginning of Beethoven Symphony No. 9, first movement.

#2 As mentioned before, RRL is the way to go around letter G for precise rhythm.

#4 After the first strike, then diminuendo slightly before making a crescendo to the last two notes, similarly in the next passage. At letter B, feel the tune in four-bar phrases with a heavy accent on the first A of the fourth bar and similarly throughout. Damp with one hand after F—it sounds really good. The trumpets and timps can add a great deal to the character by playing the passage at letter M like Figure 36.

Figure 36. Letter M, Beethoven Symphony No. 9, fourth movement.

Similarly, the last three notes before and the first note of letter O and twelve bars before letter P the same adds great effect. After letter R, shall we change it to a G? At the *allegro ma non tanto*, two huge crescendos at the eleventh bars and again later add spice and fifteen before letter T, make that *ff*. The *ff* in the ninth bar after letter T should be on the second beat, as in thirteenth bar. A big crescendo in the last couple of bars finishes the piece off nicely.

Mozart: Overture *The Magic Flute*

Just a couple of things here. We've already mentioned the pitch of the first three notes. There are exceptions to every rule and here is the first one about first beat stress. As the opera begins with the Masonic knock, should the semiquaver and minim be the same weight? For me, yes. At letter E (Figure 37), highlight the semis each time then emphasise the first beat of the third bar (Ab major chord) both times. For the following *p*, do we need to damp those three bars? You could have a damper handy on your knee and play the preceding bar RLLL to give time to put it on, then switch quickly to the Bb, then whip it off for the last five bars (again bringing out the semiquavers). But then, will anybody notice? Is it really worth the bother?

Figure 37. Letter E, Mozart's *The Magic Flute*.

Moving to the more romantic repertoire, do familiarise yourself with the melodic line and direction of all phrases. Find the places which would benefit by a "lift". Play the drums as if playing the cello, avoiding excessive body movement of course.

More romantic repertoire

Bartok:

Always have a look beforehand as many of his slow movements have the obligatory bass line

Berlioz: Symphonie Fantastique

The beginning of the last movement is best done with a totally sympathetic colleague (which I always had) on second timpani. If not, play both notes yourself.

Brahms: Symphony No. 1

#1 For the opening I used two C's, 32 and 29 to give a powerful *f*, not *ff*. As is the norm, come down a little at the 9/8 and make sure the G is stronger than the two C's. Dampers are effective after F and at H. Give a little more nine bars before H as this is for some reason without the support of the trumpets. A larger than normal *crescendo* to the last note before P is necessary (Figure 38). At the *meno allegro* I again used two C's, this time *p*.

Figure 38. Letter O-End, Brahms Symphony No. 1.

#2 Start the first rolls inaudibly. The *cresc* before F for me ended in *mf* not *p*. Watch and listen to the concert master's triplets at the end.

#4 By adding an accent at the beginning of bar 6 and similarly six bars before A is most helpful for the strings pizzicato. Two bars before B was always a long roll, slowing down at the end to match the forthcoming sextuplets. I never tried to play the 12s as written, even when requested by Barenboim. It was never effective. Make a point of the change to the C in bar 4 of B and know where the principal horn is going on the fifth bar. Carefully judged rubato is needed in this passage. You need an *mf* before the *Allegro* so the audience can hear what you are doing. Accents on all first beats in this section. Around G give the quavers their full (and a touch more) value to differentiate between them and the triplets of the strings. Seven, five and four bars before H need a noticeable *cresc* and three after H, an *mf* is recommended. At M for ten bars the first and third beats should be emphasized quite strongly. Thirteen, fifteen and sixteen after *piu allegro*, again less on the second beats. At bar 413 an F is most desirable. We must insert the traditional huge *cresc* for the last few notes of the sixes.

Symphony No. 2
#1 Starting before and finishing after the bar lines in the opening two rolls gives perfect continuation of sound. Feel the throb four and three bars before E and throughout this movement. (Figure 39)

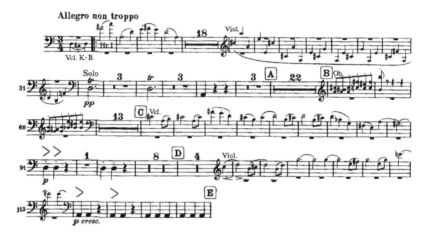

Figure 39. Beginning-E, Brahms Symphony 2, first movement.

#2 Four bars before the end, a quite strong "meaningful" stress to the first and third beats of the bar. (Figure 40)

Figure 40. Letter F-End, Brahms Symphony No. 2, second movement.

#4 Take care not to be late after the quaver rests in this movement. The last two quavers thirteen, nine, seven and eight bars before B add strength to the rhythm. A strong D eight bars before L sets the movement going again. As in Symphony No. 1, a good *cresc* on the last four notes twenty-two and eighteen before the end is exciting. (Figure 41)

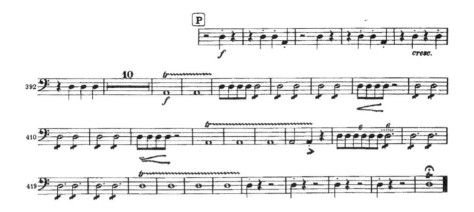

Figure 41. Letter P-End, Brahms Symphony No. 2, fourth movement.

Symphony No. 4

#1 An accent at E sets the winds off. Eight bars before F, a powerful sound to contrast with triplets elsewhere. (Figure 42)

Figure 42. Letter D-E, Brahms Symphony No. 4, first movement.

#2 Again after D, start the rolls early and finish late so there are no gaps. Listen carefully to the clarinet with the demisemiquavers at the end. (Figure 43)

Figure 43. Letter D-End, Brahms Symphony No. 4, second movement.

Ein Deutches Requiem

Great care has to be taken with the triplets, especially on the low F. It is all too easy, despite strict control, to produce no sound whatsoever on some of the notes. This is when the head is flapping about and meets the downward stroke of the stick on its way up. A harder stick than normal is helpful here.

Academic Festival Overture

Many opportunities for changing notes here. The last 3/4 passage sounds good when following the bass line. (Figure 44.)

Figure 44. *Maestoso* Brahms' Academic Festival Overture.

Britten:
Another composer to have a look at beforehand. He wrote really well for the instrument, but some works are more challenging than others.

Bruckner:
A careful choice of stick is needed in these symphonies as many start *ppp* growing to *fff* and then a solo. Slow rolls (as slow as you dare) on the lower drums help to conserve energy.

Dvořák:
So many notes changes are needed here, but it is all too easy to end up playing the bass line.

Symphony No. 5/9
#1 Nine bars after 8 should be F not E (Figure 45).

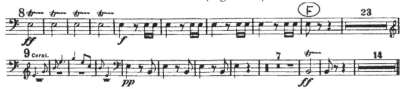

Figure 45. Fig 8-end, Dvořák Symphony No. 5, first movement.

#3 Every two bars make a slight *crescendo* going to the first beat every time and come back after the first beat. Same after 2! (Figure 46)

Figure 46. Beginning, Dvořák Symphony No. 5, second movement.

In the C major repeated section, listen carefully to the double basses as yours and their rhythms should fit together.

#4 The D quavers at 3 should be with a stronger first one. (Figure 47a) Create a pulsating feel twenty-three after 12 by giving a slight accent to each of the first quavers. How about a D for two bars five bars later? (Figure 47b) It sounds excellent.

Figure 47a. Fig 3-5, Dvořák Symphony No. 5, fourth movement.

Figure 47b. Fig 12-end, Dvořák Symphony No. 5, fourth movement.

Elgar: Enigma Variations

Var. 2 (Figure 48) Quite heavy dampers are required here,

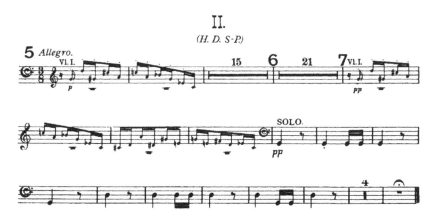

Figure 48. Variation II of Elgar's *Enigma Variations*.

Var. 4 (Figure 49) Follow the accents of the orchestra in,

Figure 49. Variation IV of Elgar's *Enigma Variations*.

Var. 9 Open the grace notes Nimrod at fig 35. Second of 36 do not *diminuendo* as the second beat is important for the suspension (Figure 50).

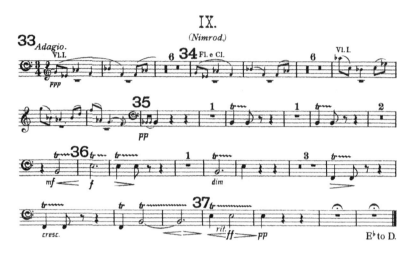

Figure 50. Variation IX of Elgar's *Enigma Variations*.

Var.13. (Figure 51) It is written for SD sticks which make life very difficult (Solti insisted on me using them and the critics commented that it was like listening to a cat on a hot tin roof, which it did). Sir Adrian liked old English pennies or half crowns, but I thought of the idea of using my fingernails. I could easily control the dynamic and it sounded as authentic as the paddle steamer it was supposed to represent in a quote from Mendelssohn's *Calm sea and prosperous voyage*. At the end, with the clarinet able to play so quietly, this was easy for me as I could bring my nails towards the rim of the drum. I would get the bass drum to hit the first note of 58 so I had time to pick up my sticks. After 60 put normal timp sticks between the legs for the quick change.

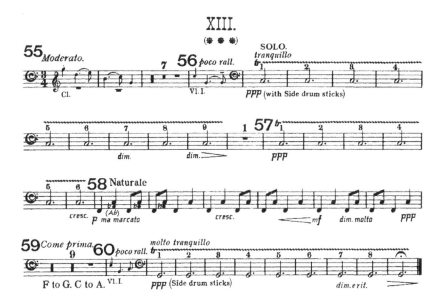

Figure 51. Variation XIII of Elgar's *Enigma Variations*.

Holst: The Planets

Why not allow the two timpanists to play the exact "tune" in "Jupiter"? (Figure 52)

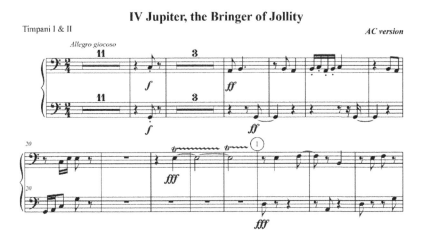

Figure 52. Beginning, Holst's *The Planets*, "Jupiter".

Janáček:

Have a good look at everything he wrote before the first rehearsal.

Rossini: William Tell Overture

A low E is very effective thunder two bars before A.

Shostakovich: Symphony No. 10

#1 Join up your rolls with the piccolo solo at the end.
#4 Cross sticking is a must at the end.

Sibelius: Symphony No. 2

#4 Add high G's at end to conserve energy.

Strauss: Don Juan

Definitely have the wooden sticks between your legs at the beginning.
Listen carefully and breathe with the oboe at the "double stopping" on D and G.
Kick brass off on B roll. Without the little accent they must rely on the conductor's beat (if there is one). (Figure 53)

Figure 53. Letter V, Strauss' *Don Juan*.

Stravinsky: Firebird Suite

Danse Infernale - Let BD do the work. Play all *sfz mf* so that stick control can be maintained with semiquavers throughout.
Finale - Huge *crescendo* into third bar of slow 7/4 at end. Very exciting with BD.

The Rite of Spring

I always liked to give my second timpanist more to play and shared the part as evenly as I could. It makes life easier and looks good.

Tchaikovsky: Romeo & Juliet Overture

A strong "heartbeat" is need at U. (Figure 54) Accent the first of every triplet and wait momentarily for the winds at the ninth bar. I found it useful to have two B's at the end for extra resonance.

Figure 54. Letter U, Tchaikovsky's Romeo & Juliet Overture.

Symphony No. 4

#1 Lead from the back in both *ben sostenuto* passages. Give every first beat an accent before K.

#2 At the second last bar you play, add a G on the second beat after the quaver A.

#3 Dampers here.

Symphony No. 5

#1 Stronger first beats at D.
A noticeable *crescendo* four bars before I and onwards and again at W. (Figure 55)

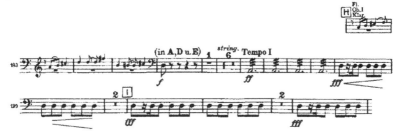

Figure 55. Letter H-I, Tchaikovsky Symphony No. 5, first movement.

At Z, I split the rolls as written except I played a single note at the beginning of the second and fourth bar. It gives the tied notes more vitality. (Figure 56)

Figure 56. Letter Z, Tchaikovsky Symphony No. 5, first movement.

#3 At O, give a heavier stress to the second beats of each bar and again after the nine bars rest. (Figure 57)

Figure 57. Letter O, Tchaikovsky Symphony No. 5, third movement.

#4 At H it's an A and twelve before B it's a C#. At the fourth bar of B, roll the second beat and give a really strong feel to the demisemiquavers on the third beat. (Figure 58)

Figure 58. Letter Bb. Tchaikovsky Symphony No. 5, fourth movement.

I omitted the E two bars before R.

Symphony No. 6

#1 Pay particular attention to the clarinet at T and go with him.

#3 Second bar of G I added an E on second quaver each time (to match the melodic line). (Figure 59)

Figure 59. Letter G, Tchaikovsky Symphony No. 6, third movement.

Verdi: Requiem

As with all his works plus Rossini, Schumann, Schubert, Mendelssohn, etc., you can leave them as they are or go way over the top (just like me).

Requiem Go with the bass line at 118 onwards? (Figure 60)

Figure 60. Bar 117-130, Verdi's Requiem.

Dies Irae

It has to be Ab at 36/38. (Figure 61a)

Figure 61a. Bar 15-25, Verdi's Requiem, Dies Irae.

At 136 How that was written as Eb and should be E natural I will never understand. (Figure 61b)

Figure 61b. Bar 133-139, Verdi's Requiem, Dies Irae.

Octave Bb's (yes, involving low Bb) in the last three bars are particularly effective.

Sanctus

There is scope for much imagination in this work, particularly with the "Sanctus" (Figure 62) where I did dreadful things. You must ensure every note is exactly in tune. No conductor, including the great Giulini, ever noticed.

Figure 62. Bar 33-74, Verdi's Requiem, Sanctus.

Libera me

Change everything b 390–95 and 2 (even 3!) C's at the end are really helpful to give maximum resonance.

Changing/adding/deleting notes

My dear colleagues, students and friends would probably expect this to be the longest and detailed chapter in my book, but it is the shortest. It is a constant battle and a highly contentious issue, certainly for me as to how far we can go to enhance the writing of so many composers who were ignorant at their time and had poor instruments at their disposal. Musical taste and discretion is needed, often not used in my case. Here are just a couple of questions.

Beethoven: Overture Egmont

Much of this is in Ab. Do we stick to F and C?

Symphony No. 5

#4 Referring to Figure 63, in bar 763, do we go with the woodwinds or with the theme of the movement or with the brass as one would normally expect?

What about the last note? Only one conductor—Stanley Pope, who shall remain nameless, featured it to encourage me to make two thunderous attacks with an exaggerated gesture of his body for the second half of the bar—it sounded ridiculous.

Figure 63. Bar 761 to the end, Beethoven Symphony No. 5, fourth movement.

Elgar: Symphony No. 1
#1 Surely the grand theme should be Ab/Db.

Bruch: Violin concerto
Two of the most essential and satisfying changes of note are in the second movement of the Bruch after the dotted rhythm which should finish on a Gb and in Beethoven 9 eighteen after G before the *allegro assai* in the fourth movement that MUST be an F natural. The drop of a major third in both cases is so powerful.

Symphony No. 2
There is a work with which you may not be familiar—Bruch's Symphony No. 2. As you will see, it starts in F and C and changes just after letter E to D and A and then before letter K reverts to F and C (Figure 64). I am sure the German publisher was unaware of his instruction at this point.

Figure 64. Bruch Symphony No. 2, first movement.

Tchaikovsky: Piano concerto

Why not play the bass line in the opening statement?

Tchaikovsky: Symphony No 3

#1 & #5 I was tempted to add the occasional extra note in Tchaikovsky Symphonies when Rostropovich was on the box. (Figures 65a-65b).

Figure 65a. Letter D-E, Tchaikovsky Symphony No. 3, first movement.

Figure 65b. Letter V-W, Tchaikovsky Symphony No. 3, first movement.

Figure 65c. Letter O-P, Tchaikovsky Symphony No. 3, last movement.

(Figure 65d) I played something closer to the Bassoon part from Letter O.

Figure 65d. Tchaikovsky Symphony No. 3, last movement *(edited)*.

Tchaikovsky: Nutcracker Suite

For me, the Waltz of the Flowers from Tchaikovsky's *Nutcracker Suite* is crying out for changes at letter B and D, to complement the Bass Trombone (Figures 66a-66b).

Figure 66a. Waltz of the Flowers from Tchaikovsky's *Nutcracker Suite*.

Figure 66b. Bass Trombone part from *Nutcracker Suite*.

And many, many more, everything from the romantic repertoire, especially European literature. I leave it to you.

The *Nutcracker Suite* took on a whole new meaning when we performed and recorded it with Leopold Stokowski in 1974 when he was ninety-two. Not the most endearing person, Stoki was far beyond his use-by-date. A person positioned between the concert master and conductor in an orchestra is invariably the soloist or occasionally an interpreter, but on this occasion it was his personal doctor, with smelling salts at the ready to provide immediate assistance, should it be necessary. A large plastic sheet was gaffer-taped under and around the podium in case of incontinence, but as far as I am aware, was still dry at the end of each session.

At one point at the rehearsal in a different venue, the caretaker's cat was released (I know not by whom) into the studio and crept about during the appropriate *"Dance of the Mirlitons"*. Apart from the three flutes and pizzicato strings, there is not much else going on, so it was not long before everyone's attention had been drawn to the inquisitive animal. With some encouragement from the bows of the front desks and to the absolute delight of the players it found its way to the front and scratched at the trousers of the maestro, who showed no reaction as his leg, along with the rest of his body, was numb.

Then the sessions at Walthamstow Town Hall, London, were like no others. After the first "take", the recording manager suggested it was played back in the studio rather than in the control room to save Stoki clambering back stage which would have incurred expensive transit time. Some players stayed in their positions and read the Daily Mail whilst others moseyed about. So, still in his high chair, he seemed at first to be listening intently with his eyes closed but it was soon apparent he was in a coma. But without warning, he suddenly burst into life and started conducting (an imaginary orchestra) and shouted "trombones", who quite understandably had left the studio. His doctor steadied him as we returned to resume the session.

This suite was at times almost unrecognisable with the ludicrously fast tempo (a lively two in a bar) chosen for the "march", creating new challenges for the double-tonguing flutes, pizzicato strings and descending scales for trombones and trumpets. The *"Dance of the Sugar Plum Fairy"* was no better with absurdly exaggerated contributions for the woodwinds, especially the bass clarinet, and an agonizingly slow arpeggiated cadenza for the celeste. The CD is currently available.

Style

I think it is safe to say that the timpanist, apart from the conductor, is the most "watched" person on the stage. I mean in concerts. It is so important to me that it is an aesthetically pleasing sight. Each player has their own style of playing and I firmly believe that no two persons should look the same, or even similar, even if they are emulating their teacher. I certainly do not want any of my pupils to look like me, and I am very sure they have no desire to look like me. My method of teaching is vastly different to that of many colleagues in other countries. All my students have characters and must play the way they choose. Once we are both happy with the "basics" as outlined above, I am happy to give them as much freedom as I can. Provided everything works and there are no major problems, then they can begin to express themselves as individuals.

I do have concerns though if they look ungainly. I attended a concert of a major symphony orchestra in the Asian region recently where the principal bassoonist demonstrated that he was really "feeling" the music. His bassoon was swaying back and forth like a large phallic pendulum. Unfortunately, the sway was not in time with the music. It was horribly off-putting and as much as I tried not to look, I couldn't help myself. We can easily distract the audience with wild or unnecessary movements, as many do. To me it is not necessary to resemble a decorator painting the ceiling after each note, or to have a fly-swatting action. Nor do we need to see the actions of European traffic cops, swimmers, jugglers or those wishing to demonstrate their karate skills. I wouldn't want the audience to think about me, "Oh, I do wish he'd stop making those ridiculous gestures". Just a pleasing style that is in keeping with the feeling of the music is all that is necessary.

The same goes for timpanists who favour one hand. The audience is led to believe the player has medical condition or an injury to the other one. The good Lord gave us two hands, so why not use two? There is no need, unless going down for a swift gin, to put the ear on the drum these days with the accuracy of the gauges, but if a check is needed, then a light tap at an appropriate time is all that's necessary. To be constantly changing sticks is also a distraction, when the same ones will do perfectly well for the most part. Our actions should complement the music, not detract from it. Smiling beatifically at the conductor is not to be recommended.

Timing

"Timing is of the essence" as they say. Full awareness is essential if your timing is to be perfect.

Every few years, when the fashion circle turns 180°, I must remind my ever conscious students that although they may attract a prospective partner, wide rimmed spectacles that shut out any peripheral vision are not to be recommended for orchestral musicians. We must have as much in our view as possible. In Hong Kong, it is common practice for people to exist in a cocoon. No seeing, looking, feeling or listening. It is not usually possible to practice at home, with the tiny apartments being filled with family, televisions at full volume and every member of the household shouting on a mobile phone. Simultaneously. It must be done elsewhere, and, as in many other musical institutions, practice rooms are at a premium, this is often difficult to achieve. The ability to listen carefully to what's going on, rather than simply hear another sound, is crucial for any musician. In ensemble playing it is compulsory.

Timing is essential in many walks of life. How many people, for example,

- stumble and shuffle before approaching a stairway, or stop completely when getting on and off the escalator?
- cause dislocation of their passengers' necks by bringing their vehicle to an abrupt stop at traffic lights?
- allow the main course to get cold whilst waiting for the vegetables to cook?
- open the car door without looking behind?
- ruin another's joke by interrupting just before the punch line?
- burn their toast and scald their mouths with boiling tea by having to rush at breakfast?
- miss their bus or plane having not packed in time?
- cause disappointment in the bedroom?

With full awareness and listening, timing becomes that much easier.
Take the opening chord of any piece of music. With the conductor's baton often providing only a scant idea of the exact moment to produce our sound, particularly with Solti, it is crucial that we look around, see the body language of the other players, listen to the breathing of the wind players, "feel" the right moment to strike the drum. Unlike double basses, clarinets and others, we cannot "creep" in.

For us, in a roll leading up to a climax, in a Mahler symphony for example, the percussionists and others are so grateful to hear the careful grading of the *crescendo*, to see our body language and so time their "back swing" with ours when we (usually) change drum.

Relationship with conductors

With the timpanist being in the enviable position of having the potential to make or break his great night, the overwhelming majority of conductors saw it that way. With the LPO, along with the other self-governing major London orchestras, any conductor who was objectionable or incompetent, was simply not invited back, unless of course he brought a string of lucrative sessions to the orchestra, when he was welcomed back with open arms. The enthusiastic Msistlav Rostropovich and Leopold Stokowski would fit well into this category. The main conductors during my time with the LPO included some of the finest musicians, and some others. Any kind of relationship with the comatose Stokowski, the fearsome George Szell and the brilliant Yevgeny Svetlanov was out of the question, but there was a host of others with whom it was a pleasure to work, including the

- consummate musician and gentleman, Sir Adrian Boult
- man sent from God, Carlo Maria Giulini
- adorable, versatile and witty Sir John Pritchard
- man unforgivably overlooked for a knighthood, Vernon Handley
- hugely talented Daniel Barenboim
- greatest Mozartian of them all, Josef Krips
- complete opposite, his waltzing brother Henry
- relaxed and generous Jesus Lopez-Cobos
- affable, thumb-licking Sir Charles Groves
- underrated, easy-going Bryden Thompson

Then there was the

- man who always "heard" tacet trumpets and timpani, Eugen Jochum
- humourless, record-one-bar-at-a-time, Walter Weller
- platform-shoed, be-toupéed, permatanned Walter Susskind
- try-even-harder-next-time James Conlon
- buffoon and bull-in-a-china-shop, Norman (Rene) del Mar
- arrogant poser with a photographic memory, Lorin Maazel
- mountebank, Zubin Mehta
- "Thanks, I'll have a whisky (a large one please)", Alexander Gibson

- chubby, boyish man in a buttoned blazer and tie, Andrew Litton
- miserable bloodhound, Erich Liensdorf
- effusive, exaggerating and forever weeping, Leonard Bernstein
- man who thought he was Solti, Edward Downes
- man who thought he was Kempe, Elgar Howarth
- man with a fireman's torch in trouser pocket, Christoph Eschenbach
- most miserable person on the planet, David Atherton
- boy from the valleys, the very Welsh Owain Arwel Hughes
- cycling vegan, Georg Tintner
- good friend of audience, bad friend of orchestra, Willi Boskovsky
- pedantic, equine Kurt Sanderling
- tongue-chewing Charles Mackerras
- man with absolutely nothing whatsoever to offer, Franz Welser-Möst
- always in the shadow of Haitink, Edo de Waart
- jolly, "is-that-OK"? ... "OK", "Oh, OK" Nicholas Braithwaite
- Sir Roger Arthur *Carver* (true) Norrington
- my hugely successful friend Sir Simon Rattle.

There were more with whom I played regularly with orchestras other than the LPO, the

- versatile, then, one-of-the-boys, Andre Previn
- frightfully proper Englishman and PSB, Sir Colin Davis
- incomparable, do it all with the stick, no need to speak, Rudolf Kempe
- "triangle too loud", Claudio Abbado
- "espressivo bass drum", size 14 shoes, Harry Blech
- suave but ineffectual Richard Bonynge
- hangman, Massimo Freccia
- unkempt Jascha Horenstein

Apart from Barenboim, Previn, Eschenbach, etc., who took up the baton with great success, there were the otherwise brilliant instrumentalists who didn't, including the

- hen-pecked, lovely, but absolutely-no-idea Yehudi Menuhin
- rude and utterly useless Dietrich Fischer-Diskau
- salivating, hopeless, "we make like spaghetti", Mstislav Rostropovich
- very mediocre, polo-necked Vladimir Ashkenazy

And the conducting composers, the

- stick insect, John Taverner
- cannot-do-anything-without-my-son's-advice, Lennox Berkeley
- difficult, morose, man of few words, misery-guts, Benjamin Britten
- man with precious few remaining brain cells, Malcolm Arnold
- flamboyant, colourful Michael Tippett

And then, more "others", the

- man with the post-prandial moist patch in his groin area, Wyn Morris
- corpulent, lolloping dugong, Arthur Davison
- much too serious, in-depth, helium fuelled voice, Loris Tjeknavorian
- bovine Igor Buketoff
- LSO fiddler who studied with Norman del Mar (!), David Measham

I have absolutely no doubt that a large number of the aforementioned adjectives would have been placed before my name. Phasing out my timp sticks over the last twenty-five years in favour of the baton, I am well aware that one white stick can do just as much damage as two brown ones.

My principal conductor to start with was Bernard Haitink and to finish Klaus Tennstedt, who were both held in the highest esteem by the members of the orchestra, and a privilege and joy with whom to make music. Interesting to note here that Klaus, who loved a drink before a show (Carlsberg special, which his wife Inge brought in large shopping bags to his dressing room), and Bernard, who did not touch a drop, an anagram of his name being "a drink in the bar". I had a lovely letter from the Tennstedts when they were told I was emigrating to Australia.

Between them was the "maestro amongst maestri". NOT. Sir Georg Solti (born Georgy Stern Solti) was a bastard. Nicholas Busch, our extraordinary, wonderful principal horn for many years described him in the exposé "The Orchestra" as *"awful—the worst conductor ever"*. He was detested by virtually every member of the LPO. His idea of making beautiful music was to encourage us to play with the shrillest, nastiest sound whenever the dynamic rose above **mp**. Bereft of any stick technique whatsoever, he was arrogant, rude and ruthless. On one occasion the rehearsal was cancelled when he was taken to hospital after stabbing himself with his baton. He had what we called "perfect ears"—no holes! In rehearsals, I must admit to being rather naughty and tuned my drums to notes that were as far removed from the required pitches as I could and hit them (at the rim or in the centre) rather louder than was required, much to the orchestra's delight. Not a flinch from the box. My colleagues encouraged me to play as forcefully as I could. Still no reaction. I mean, Mozart Jupiter symphony in Bb and high F#!

At one stage I had a drawing of the iguana created exactly in the striking position on the timpani head and the rehearsals and concerts at that time were immediately transformed into truly enjoyable experiences. On one occasion, before royalty at the Festival Hall we naturally played the national anthem. As usual, not many of us were watching, but I had to for the opening roll. When we were not distracted by the flailing arms, we realised he was conducting it in four.

At the concerts, with one shoulder forward, he would lunge towards the podium upon which he would stand convulsing, as if receiving CPR. It was reminiscent of being at London zoo, in the ape enclosure. His involuntary muscular spasms could easily have been interpreted as an up-beat, but as we all knew, there were no up-beats—they were all down with his elbows. The man was incapable of starting anything. Four preparatory beats to begin *La Boheme*! I ask you. Wholly mistimed slashes of the stick and rolling body movements resembling a crashing motorcyclist were commonplace in his performances, during which he often practised the art of gurning. The more tender passages were best likened to a snake in the final stages of sloughing. Despite having to contend with all this, the orchestra invariably played brilliantly, only for him to take all the credit and us, none.

In life, he was sandwiched between two great men, Haitink and Tennstedt, and in death between two great women, Lady Diana and Mother Teresa (who actually died on the same day). He was therefore denied the outpouring of worldly grief and the state funeral to which he was surely so rightfully entitled. Living in Australia at that time, I lost count of all the animated phone calls I received on 5 September 1997 telling me the good news. Amongst them was Stephen Trier, a wonderful musician, who, in his own words played the "clarionet" and taught at the *Royal College of Notes* in Prince Consort Road, London. He famously published that he would "dance on his grave" when GS passed away. Sadly this was not to be as Steve was taken from us far too early, but I have absolutely no doubt that he would soon have been appointed to the board of directors of the HPO (Heaven Philharmonic) to vehemently block any attempt to appoint any principal conductor of Hungarian extraction. With this notable knighted exception, I was fortunate indeed to have enjoyed an extremely good relationship with the aforementioned conductors. Do remember that all men on the box will be happy if you do not get in the way of their "unique" interpretation, but will be delighted if you can offer them that "something special".

Making music is fun

It had to be really so as to take the pressure off our intense schedule. Many people are unaware that the musicians in the four major symphony orchestras in London, LSO, LPO, PO and RPO, are all self-employed. There are NO contracts, NO fixed holidays, NO sickness benefits and importantly, NO work—NO money. It was not uncommon for us to undertake eighteen 3-hour sessions per week, many in different venues across London. Without contracts we were perfectly entitled to work with any orchestra or ensemble we chose and always did so to keep the diary full. We were busy in the concert halls and studios playing all kinds of music from classical to pop. Vast distances were covered by road and it was quite the norm for us to rehearse in the morning at Royal Festival Hall, then drive to Wembley for a film session then back again for the concert in the evening at RFH. Interestingly, when an important maestro was on the box for the RFH concerts, the orchestral notice board was hidden so that when wandering around in the breaks, they didn't see our punishing schedule. How could we possibly play Mahler symphonies to a consistently high standard after blasting away into a microphone with a click track pumping loud beats into our ears in the afternoon? But we did! We had no idea of the repertoire for film sessions and had to sight read as we received it. We gave many concerts outside London and recorded at every conceivable studio, many of them churches strewn across the capital. Any teaching and jingles had to be slotted in between. The traffic was, however, a little lighter, parking easier and there was no congestion charge when I lived there. I feel sorry for my colleagues now. This was our way of life. We knew no other.

There are so many hilarious moments in the lives of professional musicians, the following all happening at London's Royal Festival Hall.
The LPO had presented a children's concert sponsored by McDonalds on the Saturday morning. It was a special event with clowns, dancers and even Ronald himself. It concluded with the release of hundreds and hundreds of pretty helium filled balloons which quickly rose to the ceiling. The kids all left in their costumes with McMuffin vouchers and gifts. It was such a happy occasion. That evening's concert of Verdi's *Requiem* with Giulini and the Philharmonia was not. No sooner had it started, than the first balloon floated gently down and wafted above the heads of the solemn audience. This was soon followed by another, then another and come the "Dies Irae", possibly induced by the displacement of air due to the dynamic level, the entire auditorium was filling with these disturbing rubber bags. My colleagues from the Philharmonia tell me that at first they were gently brushed aside by the audience as if they were not bothersome, but before long the more

serious concert-goers became more animated, using their programs as badminton racquets and bashing them with full force as though they were shuttlecocks. It was mayhem. Giulini was in a trance as usual and seemed oblivious to the whole circus.

Whilst remembering dear Giulini, I have to very briefly recall a phrase which has "stuck". In rehearsal, with the great man on the box, Peter Chrippes was reading the Daily Mail, and missed a vital bass drum solo, causing Carlo Maria Giulini to writhe about on the podium clutching his heart, glaring at the player with laser beamed eyes and yelling "cosa?". He replied "Some you win, some you lose".

At a Sunday afternoon concert, amongst other items was as far as I remember, Alicia de Larrocha playing a Mozart piano concerto with Andre Previn on the box. What happened in the slow movement defies belief. Our principal second violinist had an unfortunate medical condition which involved spasmodic involuntary jerks of the head. It was in a quiet passage that we were suddenly aware of a violin flying through the air and crash landing by the feet of the fourth desk of firsts. Previn was dumbfounded. With an up bow at a relatively soft dynamic, one of the stronger than usual twitches had caused the point to somehow get caught between the bridge and string allowing the instrument to become airborne. Scarcely believing what he had seen, Previn covered his face as much as he could with his non-conducting hand to stifle the laughter. All eyes were on the poor principal who, whilst the other fiddle players were attempting, but failing to achieve a respectable *legato*, was sitting there twitching more violently and frequently than before with a bow in the right hand and nothing in the other. Andre did not dare to look at the poor man. By this time, he and the rest of the orchestra held their heads down to avoid embarrassment and the front rows of the audience were wondering whether it was all a set-up. A colleague at the back picked up the broken violin and decided it was in everyone's best interest to pass his good instrument to the front to allow the unfortunate man to continue. He spent the rest of the concerto in a more subdued but still jerky state.

I will finish by relating two more true stories, again at RFH and both with a demented Hungarian on the box. The LPO was scheduled to give the first performance in London of Sir Michael Tippett's symphony no 4. The work opens with "heavy breathing" which on this occasion was undertaken by the timpanist and percussion players (for which we received the obligatory "doubling" money). On paper this would seem quite simple. The first bar instructed us to take four microphones and breathe deeply whilst the sound was played through speakers around the auditorium. After lunch at the first rehearsal in a different hall, things were a little disorganized as there were no mics or equipment available to enhance the sound, but we knew that at the RFH the following morning all should be well. It was, however, not like that at all, the breathing being substituted by all manner of extraneous noises amplified by the surrounding speakers, much to the merriment of the other players. Try as we could, it was impossible to breathe as Sir Michael had instructed. We could hear our pathetic efforts magnified so greatly at the back of the hall. The screaming skull looked behind to where the sound was coming from, waving his arms and telling us to shut up, before realizing that we were in fact in front of him. He was beside himself with anger that we experienced, responsible, professional musicians, could behave in such an incompetent and puerile manner and be wholly unable to perform such a basic task. He referred to us as "silly babies". Every member of the orchestra knew what was in store for the evening concert, which the BBC had decided to broadcast. The four of us had sensibly discussed the real probability of a monumental disaster, so agreed to put the proverbial blinkers on and stare straight ahead rather than having any contact with our adjacent colleague. The audience sitting behind us knew that this work was a little out of the ordinary with hand held microphones placed on a high stool in front of each of us. Walking onto the stage, I did not dare to look at my mates. In fact I looked in the opposite direction. The Neanderthal man appeared and we waited for silence. Each of us picked up our microphone and made absolutely sure it was not switched on until the last possible moment, and then waited for the involuntary twitch to signal our first inhalation. Out of the corner of my eye, I noticed that one of the boys was leaning forwards to try and hide his face. Instead of the required insufflations of breath there was at first stifled tittering which was soon followed by panting, snorting and various other noises booming around the hall. All around us we were aware of muffled laughter from the audience as well as from the other players. Three of us had the presence of mind to switch off our microphones before the BBC cut the current. The "skull" gave us the "death stare". How we ever recovered to play our customary instruments I will never know. In fact, we didn't. Colleagues in other orchestras will have been greatly relieved to note that in subsequent performances the breathing is pre-recorded.

The other unforgettable one concerned a performance of Hans Werner Henze's tone poem *Heliogabalus Imperator*. This piece was written for Solti and the Chicago Symphony, but as was the usual custom with large scale works, our major conductors would "practise" the piece on us then take the experience to their other orchestra, or occasionally, with the exception of

GS, the other way around. For this performance, in addition to my timpani, I was asked to "play" the lion's roar, a peculiar construction of wood in the shape of a drum, animal skin and a length of cord. There is a hole in the middle of the "head" through which to thread the cord and a knot at one end to prevent it following through. With the string stretched as tightly as possible with one hand, a sticky cloth is applied with the other and pulled sharply upwards to allow the skin to resound as in the roar of a lion.

It rarely happened that I was called upon to play percussion in the orchestra but with my colleagues all occupied at these relevant places in the score, the job fell to me. Already with five timpani around me, space was at a premium and to find an appropriate spot for the lion's roar was not easy considering it had to be straddled to keep the instrument anchored to the floor. The rehearsals went as well as could be expected, with the predictable comments and jungle noises coming mainly from the wind players. Many out-of-the-ordinary instruments are required in this piece, including the flexatone, bird calls, whistles, steel drums, boo-bams and thunder sheet. There were two "solos" for the lion's roar.

All was well at the beginning of the performance. The audience didn't seem to care much for the piece until the first of my solos. Astride my instrument waiting for the first cue I was well prepared having given the cloth a healthy rubbing of double bass rosin. As GS looked over, I pulled hard on the string, when the instrument broke with a sickening crack from its moorings and the knot went clean through the skin of the drum resulting, instead of a roaring sound, a little "pop", heard only by me, the percussionists and the audience behind. There was just silence. He made a frenzied gesture in my direction indicating I should make a far greater sound, but all I had in my hand was a flaccid string with a knot at the end. I held it up hoping he would realise what had happened, but of course he knew absolutely nothing about the construction of such an instrument. He simply blamed me for missing the cue. Then with horror, I realised I had to repeat the exercise a little later on. There was no time or room for me to upturn the drum and re-thread it. What was I to do? Dreading the consequences, I waited for the cue. The reptile had already looked towards me to see if I was ready and I crouched down in the "set-up" position having again visibly rosined the unattached cord. I could see all the percs to my right watching and wondering what I had in mind. There was only one thing. I went through the motion of actually playing the thing. As I jerked the limp string upwards, I let out, as loudly as I could, a grrrrrrrr sound. That was it. Solti stared at me in utter disbelief and the whole place fell apart including the percs who were hiding behind the large bass drums, tam-tams and the thunder sheet so they couldn't be seen (Keith Millar, normally the stalwart principal of the section was completely helpless). The audience behind us was laughing loudly and the rest of the orchestra was in hysterics. My head was bowed but as I had to wait for a double bass cue to begin the timpani cadenza, I couldn't disappear completely. I waited for the cue. It didn't happen. The entire bass section was cowering behind their instruments unable to put bow to string. I couldn't help noticing a desperate waving gesticulation from the box in my direction that I should by now have started playing my cadenza. I had really lost track of what was happening and so played anything that came to mind. The gibbon soon gave me the abundantly clear impression that I should stop. So I did and there was again silence, except for the pianissimo high pitched bird sounds coming from the flutes and the louder muted laughter from those behind the thunder sheet. At that point, whilst doubled over in a listless condition, Kevin Nutty's cigarette lighter fell from his top pocket and bobbled down to the riser below, causing even greater disruption to the performance, which was already in tatters. Michael Frye's face, alarmingly red for some time had turned puce, and we feared for his life. Desperately trying to compose myself at the end after the constant distractions that had riddled the premiere of the work, I was, through my tired and glazed eyes, vaguely aware of what appeared to be a bald eagle in tails flapping around on the podium in a fruitless attempt to coordinate its movements. I gathered myself hoping that it would simply fly away, but upon refocussing realized that this was impossible as it had two broken wings. Apart from the occasional bodily spasm the forlorn creature remained in a pitiful condition for the remainder of the performance. *SUCH IS LIFE!*

I was recently asked to be interviewed by BBCTV for a program entitled "Solti—Maestro or Mephisto". I jumped at the opportunity. My first question was, "Alan, into which category would you put Sir Georg?" My answer was "the latter". Upon checking this book prior to publication, I realised that quite a number of pages contained the words Georg Solti. I reflect with great satisfaction on the occasionally turbulent, but very often comical and in the case of the lion's roar episode, side-splitting experiences we shared. I thank Sir Georg for being with us to enjoy these diverse and sometimes absurd situations, most of which my colleagues and I found to be hilarious, whereas he didn't. These unthinkable events could never have happened at the Eastern Electricity Board and should never have happened on the stage at RFH but they did and are unforgettable.

He spent many years trying to teach us all the things we should do and all those we shouldn't do in order to become fine orchestral players. Sadly, he failed as all his ideas fell into the "should not do" box.

Now with more time on his hands Sir Georg may choose to study the real art of conducting, although somehow I doubt it, so that when we next meet, I need just the one up beat.

ALL THAT ASIDE, THANK YOU GEORGY STERN SOLTI
FOR ENRICHING MY LIFE

Alan Cumberland, Hong Kong, September 2014

PHOTO CREDITS

Acknowledgements and thanks are due to the estate of Alan Cumberland (1A, 1B, 2A, 2B, 3A, 3B, 4A, 4B, 5A, 6A, 7A, 7B, 7C, 8A, 8B, 9A, 9B, 10A, 10B, 11B, 13B, 15, 16A, 16B, 16C,17A, 20A, 20B, Back cover Alan Cumberland *B &W* 1969); The National Theatre (5B, *"Love for Love"* 1965); Glyndebourne Festival Programme 1985 (6B, "Wooden Sticks"); London Philharmonic Yearbook 1985 (11A,"Sunburnt in Perth"); Susan Vick, (12A, Qld Conservatorium Percussion Ensemble 1989); Lucas Gordon (12B, Qld Conservatorium Percussion Ensemble 1994);
Brett Carvolth, (13A, LPO Concert Programmes); David Morbey (14, David Morbey Timpani sticks); (17B Lions roar) Courtesy of Nathan Hubbard; London Philharmonic Orchestra (18, LPO Royal Festival Hall *Photo by Terry Hall*); Laurence Reese (19, "Final LPO Concert, April 1987. 21A, *"Life is for Living"*, "Brisbane 2009, 21B, *"Pillars of Society"* Brisbane 2009.)
Cover photo and design by Brett Carvolth. Inset photos unknown (Boult, Haitink, Tennstedt, Pritchard, Giulini, Solti); Anuwat Nakpawan, Princess Galyani Vadhana Institue of Music, Bangkok (Back cover photo. AC conducting, Bangkok 2014); Back Cover B & W "Young Alan" unknown; *"The Special Timpanist"* photo Courtesy of David Morbey. *Photo by Peter Musson*, Qld Conservatorium 1988. Appendix photo courtesy of Southern Percussion, UK. Back Cover *"Bartok"* review originally published by Hi Fi News and Record Vol 16 December 1971. *"Perlman"* review source unknown.

All musical excerpts were taken from the author's personal library and collection accumulated over many years. Some original sources are therefore unknown.

NOTES

Compositions by Alan Cumberland.

20 Graduated Studies for Timpani
Two Challenges for Timpani
11 Graduated Studies for Snare Drum

Available from:
Southern Percussion
Elmwood, The Drive, Rayleigh
Essex, SS6 8XQ UK

ABOUT THE AUTHOR

British born Alan Cumberland studied piano and violin from an early age and added percussion to these in his teens. He performed with all the major symphony orchestras in London and was invited to join the London Philharmonic Orchestra with whom he remained as principal timpanist for twenty years. He was a member of the Board of Directors for nine years. With the LPO, he made numerous recordings for television, film and disc and undertook many world tours. The orchestra's principal conductors during that time were Haitink, Solti and Tennstedt, with annual guest appearances by Barenboim, Boult, A Davis, Eschenbach, Giulini, Handley, Horenstein, Jochum, Krips, Maazel, Marriner, Pritchard, Rattle, Rostropovitch, Sanderling, Stokowski , Svetlanov and de Waart. With the LPO and other London orchestras, he worked regularly with Abbado, Barbirolli, Bernstein, Britten, Copland, C Davis, Fruhbeck de Burgos, Horenstein, Markevitch, Mehta, Previn, M Shostakovich, Szell and a host of others. Legendary soloists included Accardo, Allen, Arrau, Ashkenazy, Bachauer, J Baker, Brendel, Carreras, Curzon, Domingo, Fischer-Dieskau, Galway, Gedda, Haendel, R Hunter, te Kanawa, Kempff, Kennedy, Kremer, Lupu, Menuhin, Milstein, Nelsova, J Norman, D and I Oistrakh, Pauk, Pavarotti, Perlman, Perahia, du Pre, Rostropovitch, Rubinstein, Sills, Stern, Szeryng, Sutherland, Tortelier, Zukerman and so many more. He was also Professor of Timpani at the Royal College of Music from 1970 and examiner for the Royal Schools and Trinity College London. He held master classes on a regular basis in Europe, USA, Asia and Australia. In 1987, he was offered a post at the Queensland Conservatorium, Australia and for the next 11 years was Senior Lecturer in Timpani and Percussion, Resident Conductor of the Conservatorium Symphony Orchestra and Principal of the Young Conservatorium. He was the Chairman of the Queensland Percussion Panel of the Australian Music Examinations Board. He also conducted the Queensland Symphony and Queensland Philharmonic Orchestras. He was invited to perform as principal timpanist with the World Philharmonic Orchestra in Bangkok in 1996 to perform the first symphony of Mahler before King Bhumipol and has returned to Thailand on many occasions to coach members of the Bangkok Symphony Orchestra and to give master classes for timpani and percussion students. Alan Cumberland joined the staff of The Hong Kong Academy for Performing Arts in September 1998 as Head of Woodwind, Brass and Percussion, and is Resident Conductor of the Academy Symphony Orchestra. He directed the orchestra in Spain, France and England and has conducted twelve operas and the hit show 'Fiddler on the Roof' at the Academy. Alan retired in September 2015 and moved to North Lakes, Qld Australia to be with his family.

SELECTED LIST OF RECORDINGS

Some examples discussed in this book can be found within the following list.
Catalogue numbers denote original CD release.

Abbreviations
LPO London Philharmonic Orchestra
NPO National Philharmonic Orchestra

BRAHMS Symphony No. 1	LPO / Tennstedt	EMI CDC 7 47029 2 Recorded 1984
BEETHOVEN Symphonies 1- 9	LPO / Haitink	DECCA DN0027 Recorded 1974-76
BEETHOVEN Symphonies 9 in D Minor	LPO / Tennstedt	BBCL 4131-2 Recorded Live 1985
BEETHOVEN Overtures	LPO / Tennstedt	EMI CDC 7 47086 2 Recorded 1984
BRAHMS Academic Festival Overture Symphonies 1-3	LPO / Jochum	EMI 7243 5695152 5 Recorded 1976
BRAHMS Ein Deutches Requeim	LPO / Tennstedt	EMI 7243 5695182 2 Recorded 1984
DVOŘÁK Symphonies 1 - 9	LPO / Rostropovich	EMI 7243 56570528 Recorded 1979-1980
ELGAR Enigma Variations Op. 47	LPO / Haitink	LPO 0002 Recorded Live 1986
ELGAR Symphony No. 1 Op.55	LPO / Handley	EMI CDB 7 62036 2 Recorded 1979
HOLST The Planets	LPO / Boult	EMI CDM 7 69045 2 Recorded 1979
MAHLER Symphonies 1-9 Complete Recordings	LPO / Tennstedt	EMI 0944932
MOZART Overtures	LPO / Haitink	PHILIPS 432 512-2

PUCCINI
La Boheme
Domingo★ Caballe

LPO / Solti

SONY 88697579022
Recorded 1974

PUCCINI
Turandot
Pavarotti★ Sutherland

LPO / Mehta

DECCA 414 274 2
Recorded 1972

SHOSTAKOVICH
Symphony No. 10

LPO / Haitink

DECCA 425 064-2
Recorded 1977

STRAUSS
Don Juan

LPO / Rickenbacher

EMI CDB 7 67447 2
Recorded 1985

STRAUSS
Waltzes from
Der Rosenkavalier

LPO / Del Mar

EMI CDB 7 62632 2
Recorded 1979

STRAVINSKY
Firebird

LPO / Solti

LPO 0025
Recorded Live 1985

STRAVINSKY
The Rite of Spring

LPO / Haitink

PHILIPS 420 491-2

TCHAIKOVSKY
Romeo and Juliet Overture
Symphonies 1- 6

LPO / Rostropovich

EMI 7243 565709 2 4
Warner 9029586924
Recorded 1977-1978

TCHAIKOVSKY
Symphony No. 5

LPO / Baitiz

ASV CD QS6097

TCHAIKOVSKY
Piano Concerto ★ Fowke

LPO / Boettcher

EMI CDB 762009 2
Recorded 1984

TCHAIKOVSKY
"Nutcracker Suite"

LPO / Stokowski

PHILIPS 442 735-2
Pentatone 5186229

TCHAIKOVSKY
Complete Ballets
Swan Lake ★ Nutcracker★
Sleeping Beauty

NPO / Bonynge

DECCA 460 411-2

VERDI
Requiem

LPO /
J Lopez-Cobos

LPO 0048
Recorded Live 1983

INDEX

APPENDIX

ALAN ROY CUMBERLAND
02/09/1945 - 4/12/2016

This book was written in September 2014 in Hong Kong. Sadly Alan passed away peacefully on December 4, 2016 surrounded by family and friends after a long illness and before a final version of this book could be completed. It was his desire to share his experiences, vast knowledge and passion for music and life with as many as possible.

He is survived by loving partner Sandy Leung, dearly beloved Helen Cumberland, daughters Annette & Lisa and adorable grandchildren, Chloe and Ella. Alan was an exceptional musician, an inspirational teacher, mentor and friend to many.

"LIFE IS FOR LIVING"

Made in the USA
Monee, IL
26 August 2021

76578580R00085